C000276314

GHOSTBUSTERS UK

To protect the identity of those people who wish to remain anonymous, we have used forenames only. Where a surname is used, however, the name is genuine.

GHOSTBUSTERS UK

ROBIN FURMAN
and
MOIRA MARTINGALE

ROBERT HALE · LONDON

© *Robin Furman and Moira Martingale 1991*
First published in Great Britain 1991

ISBN 0 7090 4433 X

Robert Hale Limited
Clerkenwell House
Clerkenwell Green
London EC1R 0HT

Photoset in North Wales by
Derek Doyle & Associates, Mold, Clwyd.
Printed in Great Britain by
St Edmundsbury Press, Bury St Edmunds, Suffolk
and bound by WBC Bookbinders Ltd, Bridgend, Glamorgan.

Contents

Illustrations

Between pages 96 and 97

PICTURE CREDITS

R.L. Carter: 11; David Bocking: 13.

Foreword

by Uri Geller

Most people believe in ghosts. Whether they are prepared to admit it or not is another matter, but in any mixed company of adults, there will be several with a tale to tell of the paranormal. There may follow debate and argument between believers and sceptics, but one thing is certain: ghosts cannot simply be ignored.

There has never been a period in human history without its ghosts. Tales of ghosts are passed down from generation to generation. In a sense, a civilization may be judged by its ghosts.

But whether they are sombre, frightening, happy or angry spirits, ghosts in all their variety deserve to be studied. We need to understand this shadowy and mysterious world of the supernatural.

With a serious but light touch, Robin Furman and the team of Ghostbusters UK reveal the true stories about their other-worldly experiences. For believers or unbelievers, these ghostbusting tales from the team's casebook should not be missed.

Introduction

The first ghost I ever saw appeared on the landing of my house in Grimsby about twenty years ago. It's a big, old house in a place known locally as Nun's Corner, because there is a theological history to the site, going back to the eleventh century. I suppose, in view of that, I should not have been surprised to find a ghostly nun in the house.

At the time, I was a businessman and I had no great interest in the paranormal. On this particular evening, I was going upstairs and I thought I noticed a movement on the landing. At first I thought it might be one of the children – but they were in bed. Then I reached the top of the stairs and there she was: a tall nun. I could see her quite clearly and she looked completely real. It was only when I saw her face that I realized she wasn't real … because she hadn't got one. In its place was a glowing light. I was absolutely amazed, of course. She was wearing an old-fashioned head-dress, whereas modern nuns have flat head-dresses. Then she drifted away and was gone. It all happened so quickly that I didn't have time to be scared. I was utterly astounded and registered the same kind of shock that I would have felt had I seen a strange man or an animal on the landing. It was not true fear – I certainly was not afraid that she was going to do me an injury – but it was fear of the unknown. I went cold.

Downstairs Sheila, my wife, was sitting watching television. 'What's the matter with you?' she asked when I walked in.

What was I going to say? She was certain to think I was

11

mad if I told her. 'Why?' I parried, trying to be casual.

'You look as if you've seen a ghost!' she said.

Since then, our nun has reappeared a few times – my daughter Victoria found her sitting on the end of the bed once – and the nun certainly fuelled my interest in the paranormal. But I could not have guessed then that one day I would be leading possibly the world's only team of amateur ghostbusters! What sort of job was that for a respectable businessman? And what would my father, Louie Furman, have thought of it all? On reflection, he would probably have registered only mild surprise. He was hardly a conventional father, being a well-known jockey who rode in the Grand National several times. He taught me to ride before I could walk. I'm convinced my father was psychotic – to put a four-year-old on a racehorse is not funny. But it did mean that physical pursuits came naturally to me and not being very tall, I did 'wiry' things. For instance, I count 'judo instructor' among my list of occupations when compiling a CV. Add to that psychiatric nurse, lumberjack, insurance salesman, night-club pianist, poet and milkman – and you can see that being a ghostbuster is not such an unusual career for me!

I used to write a 'magic' column for the local newspaper. That was my interest – everything from ancient Egypt to modern parapsychology. I was never interested in stage magic and sleight-of-hand stuff. What fascinated me was *real* magic – witches and voodoo. For instance, if we believe faith-healing can work, then so can curses. Kill or cure. As a teenager I became interested in hypnosis. I was seventeen when I hypnotized my first person – actually, it was Joyce, the family maid, and I was so astounded that I had managed it that I ran through the house to tell my parents: 'Look, I've hypnotized Joyce!' I used the traditional method: 'Your eyes are getting heavy' – and so on. I just copied it out of a book and discovered I had a gift. After that I was terribly popular at parties, hypnotizing people, but as time went on the novelty wore off and I forgot about it. Later I began to be interested in more complicated hypnotic processes, such as hypnotizing people from a distance, without their knowledge.

I took my degree in psychology and philosophy at Hull University as a mature student, and then as well as practising hypnotherapy, I began lecturing on psychology, hypnosis and parapsychology at local colleges. The Ghostbusters arose spontaneously out of this. I used to talk about psychic research to my students and one evening after a lecture we were having a pint or six in the Harvest Moon pub in Grimsby and I started to tell them about one of my cases: a local night-club owner and his wife were having a spot of bother with a poltergeist at their home. It was the usual sort of poltergeist effect: footsteps were heard on the stairs, doors opened and closed of their own accord, lights went on and off, objects were moved around – including a knife which had jumped off a table when no one had been near it. But there was a slight difference: this poltergeist apparently enjoyed throwing parties. The woman had been terrified when she had woken after retiring to bed for an early night, to hear the sound of a party going on in the empty room next to hers. She heard the tinkle of glasses, the noise of chairs being moved across the floor and the muffled sound of voices belonging to a considerable number of people. She got out of bed and went to the door of the empty bedroom to listen to the noise inside – but she didn't dare go in for fear of what she might find.

'Actually, I could do with a bit of assistance on this one,' I happened to mention to Rodney Mitchell, Janice Paterson and the rest. There was a chorus of volunteers and in the end, seven of us went on the expedition to that old cottage. That's when the thought first hit me: we made quite a team. There was Janice, who is a microbiologist; Andy Butterworth, a photographer; Rodney Mitchell, a computer consultant; Stephen Morley, an electronics engineer; Russell Whitwell, another computer boffin; my son Andy and myself. Apart from Rodney, Janice and my son Andy, the other people have since become involved in different things, but on that occasion we all went off to the haunting for the first time in Andy's big black car – the 1959 Austin Princess, an ex-mayoral limousine which was to become our famous Ghostmobile. And the answer is, no, we don't have a number plate ECTO 1 like the Ghostbusters in the film! More requests came in and we became known locally. Then the *Ghostbusters* film was released – and that was how we became known as the Grimsby Ghostbusters. We did not set out to say: 'We'll be Ghostbusters, like in the film,' but to paraphrase the words from the film-score, there's something strange in everyone's neighbourhood. You'd be surprised how much there is about. Who were the people in Grimsby going to call?

What exactly happens when the Ghostbusters are called out? Well, firstly, we have to establish if what is happening to the person is physical or psychological. You have to be a professional. When I was reading for my degree I specialized in remedial psychotherapy and, having had some previous success with hypnosis – albeit for entertainment and fun – I grew increasingly fascinated by the therapeutic applications of hypnosis. My early attempts at entering the field of medicine had been varied. Having abandoned reading for a medical degree – thanks to my execrable maths! – I had gone on to work in various hospitals throughout the country, qualifying as a psychiatric nurse and then as a laboratory technician. Because of my consuming interest in the psychology of the brain, I worked in the laboratory and the mortuary of a large mental hospital, involved in brain extirpation – the study of the biology of the brain of diseased mental patients.

I also became involved in group therapy and studied the works of Freud, Jung and other psychoanalytical masters. This, in turn, led me to study counselling – and I believe that this has helped me come to terms with and overcome many of my own problems, while also giving me considerable insight into the problems of others. While at the hospital I had the opportunity to study narco-hypnosis, which is the use of a drug – often pentothal in those days – to induce the trance-like condition which is sometimes helpful in studying a patient's condition. Hypnotic techniques can be used in a variety of ways. For demonstration purposes, I could hypnotize, or otherwise relax, a roomful of students at one of my evening classes. More properly these days, I use the techniques in individual sessions wih clients. So you see, I have devoted more than twenty years to this, and the background knowledge comes into play when I am trying to ascertain whether there truly are genuinely physical effects being felt in a situation, or whether there is a psychological cause which needs the attention of a psychologist or a psychiatrist, rather than a parapsychological investigator.

To give an example, we went to see one very nice man and in our preliminary investigations we noticed that his house smelt very strongly of what we thought was disinfectant. 'What's been going on?' we asked and he said he was being physically attacked by disembodied entities. Now, I believe that this phenomenon is possible, so I was quite prepared to accept his story. I was soon to be disillusioned, for he suddenly shouted: 'Look, there's one now! There it is! I'll get it!' Then he got out a giant can of fly spray and started squirting it around. 'There! That's got it!' he cried, and leaned towards me confidentially. 'I get them like that, you know.' He had cans of fly spray in his house, in his car – everywhere! He was obviously hallucinating. It was clearly a psychological case.

We always try to search for a logical solution first. People sometimes say to me: 'Oh, you believe in ghosts, do you?' and I usually reply in an offhand way: 'Not particularly.' But certainly, I saw a nun on the landing and I'm not going to pretend, out of fear of being thought mad, that I did not. We research ghosts out of interest and to help the people concerned, who are often very worried and frightened. One woman rang the Social Services and said: 'I think I'm haunted,' and they put her in touch with me, thinking she was nutty. But she was not nutty; she *was* haunted – and we settled it in one session.

Some people think we're eccentrics, but we're not particularly concerned about what people think. They can believe what they like, although personally, I have no belief system at all. Correction: if I have one, it's a belief that I don't have a belief system! Our theories? Ah well, theory of every type is all very good, but it doesn't stop things from existing. There may be a rational explanation for all paranormal events, but it may not yet be within our sphere of knowledge.

Amongst our equipment we now have a splendid ghost-detecting machine – we call it the Roboghost – which is really an Acorn computer that picks us slight changes in temperature, light and vibration, but our equipment is mainly for monitoring. We don't go out to zap ghosts with proton guns. That stuff is just for the box office. Our methods may not be considered rational by everyone, but who's to say that just because science cannot yet find a rational explanation for a mysterious happening, there *is* no rational explanation? Nevertheless, the cry of the scientists is still: 'Proof!'

One of my favourite scholars of the eighteenth century is Dr Samuel Johnson. He was fascinated by magic, too – and he had something to say about the proof that scientists always demand. 'As to ghosts,' he declared, 'all proof's against it ... and all belief's for it.'

1

Enter the Ghost...

It was a hell of a night for a ghost-hunt.

A filthy wet night – one of those wild March nights on the east coast of England which chills to the core. We were huddled together in our ghostmobile, battling with the violent elements to reach a remote cottage somewhere in the wilds of Louth, Lincolnshire. Even though we were equipped with a map, these winding country roads had a labyrinthian quality in the solid darkness – and who was to know what spooks were waiting for us at Sandra and Roland Holland's lonely house?

Sandra had telephoned me in desperation after a Roman Catholic priest and a Methodist minister had turned deaf ears to her pleas. Exorcism wasn't exactly up their street, the men of the cloth had said. The Hollands were farmworkers and the whole family was in a blue funk because they had been told by their farmer employer that they must move house. They must leave their cosy little cottage and move to another home: Grange Farm. The hundred-year-old Grange Farm was larger than their present house but it had, they believed, an unwelcome visitor in residence. Ghost? Poltergeist? Let's just call it a presence; an oppressive 'something' that had possession of the house – and affected the people within it. Fearsome events had occurred at Grange Farm – events that tax one's belief in coincidence: sudden deaths, strange and bizarre accidents, numerous instances of terminal illness which had afflicted many previous occupants. The last couple to move into Grange Farm had fled after only one night, abandoning their jobs on the land. Sandra had told me about it.

'They said it was a funny house and they couldn't sleep. Then another couple came and the wife refused to set foot inside the door.' Sandra's voice became edgy. 'People have accidents here. The last people to live here for any length of time ... the man electrocuted himself. The family wouldn't live here after that. The people who were here before them, the mother and her daughter both died suddenly of cancer – and the daughter was only a young girl. And then the husband got pulled into the threshing machine ...'

On the other end of the phone Sandra became silent. Perhaps she expected a reaction of disbelief from me. Ah, no. It is easy to scoff and cry: 'Superstition!' Those people who laugh might not laugh quite so readily if it was they who had to live in this house – as Sandra and Roland would have to. The thought filled them with terror, but to refuse would mean relinquishing their jobs, as previous people had. The Hollands had first-hand experience of the house because of a friendship with some previous occupants. Sandra had been there, having a coffee, when she heard footsteps crossing the kitchen ceiling. There was no one upstairs. Sandra had felt the cold in the atmosphere and her son's girlfriend had pledged never to enter the house again after she felt someone – some*thing* – pushing her as she stood alone near the top of the stairs.

'The priest and the minister thought I was a bit potty,' Sandra had said on the phone. 'It was my son Kenneth who said "Why don't you call in the Ghostbusters"?'

So here we were, the motley crew who made up the Grimsby Ghostbusters, racing round to inspect a spectre again – and the weather was straight out of a Hammer horror film! Janice squinted at the map. 'Try a left here,' she instructed and my son Andy, who both drives and cares for our ghostmobile, swung the big car around. The headlight-beams swayed through the sheets of rain and we bumped our way into an unadopted road, pitted with pot-holes. Water and mud splashed up from the tyres. A right turn took us to the house at the end of another narrow lane.

We emerged from the car to feel the rain and wind whipping us bitterly, flattening my jeans against my shins, flapping coats, making eyes water and cheeks sting. Strong gusts rattled through the bare trees which formed a copse alongside the house. At the heart of the gloomy spinney, we were to learn, was an old duck-pond, lying deep, silent and stagnant, with greasy scum and green moss resting on its surface. Sandra Holland opened the front door of Grange Farm. A robust woman in spectacles, wearing jeans and trainers, she did not look the sort to be easily scared. A staircase ran up opposite the front door, but the gang and I followed Sandra as she turned left through a small parlour to the large room where most of the paranormal effects had been experienced. The team and I are rarely nervous on our ghostbusting missions and our mood was one of enthusiastic anticipation as Sandra turned the door-handle into the empty room.

The door would not budge. 'That's funny,' said Sandra. 'I was in here a minute ago.' She turned the handle harder and pushed at the door. Closed. Jammed shut. Just as if someone on the other side had wedged their shoulder against it.

'Let me try,' said Andy, the nearest we have to Desperate Dan. Alone, he failed, so together we all heaved at the door. Suddenly it opened and we tumbled into the room. This room ran from the front to the back of the house, with a window at either end. The lights were on and the gas fire was lit, but it was cold; colder than it was outside the house. The atmosphere was very unpleasant and there was a fusty smell; smells are often associated with poltergeist effects. 'Shut-up and claustrophobic' was how Sandra had described the atmosphere in the house – and she was right.

'I'll just take a look upstairs,' said Rodney. He ambled out of the room and up the stairs. Janice shivered and Stephen, who had been pottering around taking temperature readings, glanced up. 'The temperature's well down,' he noted. Janice and I rubbed our frozen hands. He didn't need to tell *us*!

'Sometimes we hear footsteps overhead – especially when we're in the kitchen,' said Sandra, 'and we often hear them going upstairs on the other side of that wall.' With a nod, she indicated the opposite, long wall.

'And what's on the other side of that wall?' I asked.

She shrugged. 'Nothing. It's the end wall of the house.' Grange Farm was detached. Only fresh air and darkness lay beyond the wall. Or did it?

Rodney returned. 'It really feels weird here – particularly upstairs. It's so oppressive.'

'Yes,' I agreed, after we had toured the inside of Grange Farm. 'Maybe there's something here. We'll have to do something – preferably in the daylight. How does tomorrow suit you?' Sandra looked relieved. A time was set. Armed with our equipment, we would return the next day to grapple with the ghost.

What we weren't to know until the following day's exploration was that immediately behind that gable-end wall of the lounge – the wall where the footsteps were heard – there was not the fresh air of the Louth countryside, as we had all believed. Our first action was to investigate the house with all its nooks and crannies. Covered with grime, high up on the wall at the back of the house – alongside the rear picture-window of the lounge – was a small window. We climbed up to see through it and what we saw astonished us. There, to our surprise, was a narrow staircase, apparently blocked in at both the top and the bottom. Excitedly, we raced upstairs to the bedroom where, by rights, the staircase should have emerged. Nothing. The wall was smooth and there was no suggestion of a door ever having been there, although clearly there must have been access at some time. Sandra was puzzled. She had known previous tenants and none had seemed to know about the secret staircase which contained no way in or out. Yet they had heard those footsteps clattering up and down it, too. The chance that there might be a paranormal presence or entity became stronger.

Until then I was quite keen on the ley-lines theory to explain the Grange Farm mystery. Ley lines are paths of energy which were first drawn to our attention in Britain by Alfred Watkins in 1921. Before this, the ancient Chinese believed that such 'invisible' paths crossed their country. They considered it unwise to build at points where these paths – called *lung meis* or 'dragon paths' – crossed. In Britain, Watkins believed, ley lines connect all the holy sites in the country – lines of magnetic force underground. There is evidence that birds and animals use these magnetic lines for homing. If a house is built over a nodal point where the ley lines cross, one belief is that there are many energies to the fore which can have an unpleasant effect on the people living there: illness, disorientation and sleeplessness can occur. There is a theory that at these points a 'magnetic vortex' might somehow 'record' past events and cause those events (for example, a battle) to impinge on the present. So ley lines seemed a likely explanation for the strange goings-on at Grange Farm. Until we found the secret staircase, that is.

Clearly there were some forces emanating from that staircase. Even Ben, my Newfoundland dog who went along with us, showed an interest in the haunted staircase. We therefore decided to tackle Grange Farm in two ways: to deal with the effects of the earth energies which may have been unpleasant in the house and to exorcize any effects which emanated from the hidden staircase. We collected our ghostbusting equipment from the car. Now, the Ghostbusters of the movie might use electric ray-guns, ghost-traps and other zapping paraphernalia, but our gear for the purpose in hand was a little simpler. We took from the car a long rope, some chalk, some cardboard pyramids and several other small items. Then we went to work.

Our first task was to disrupt the earth's magnetic forces around the house, so we took our rope and completely encircled Grange Farm. The rope was no ordinary rope. Entwined in it was a flexible wire so that when the two ends met it formed a continuous, unbroken circle. This formed a 'ring of power'– a shape that has historically been found effective against unpleasant forces.

In the daylight the stagnant pool at the side of the house looked a little less threatening. We carried the rope past the pool, across the land behind the house, around the other side and back to the front door, completing the circle. We could have gone further: a traditional way of disturbing electromagnetic waves is by burying metal – knocking bent nails into the ground. At the four points of the compass we erected cardboard pyramids. Why the pyramids? Well, there is some evidence that 'shape' seems to produce its own effect. I do not believe that anyone understands thoroughly the mechanics of this, any more than we know the wavelength of a poltergeist. But we know that poltergeist effects exist and we know of their associations with certain people. We know the poltergeist energies come from the unconscious part of the brain. We just don't know how.

Pyramids are particularly interesting in the way they can affect the electromagnetism of the earth. There is a fascinating true story about a team of scientists from the USA who, in 1968, conducted archaeological investigations, together with a team from the Ein Shams University in Cairo, at the Great Pyramid of Cheops, where the Pharaoh Kufu is buried. They were trying to find further chambers within the pyramid, using electronic counters. These worked by passing a ray of energy through solid walls and floors around the base of the pyramid, which covers some twelve acres. Obviously, a ray takes longer to pass through solid matter than it does to pass through space, so if the tape-recordings on the equipment registered a slow–quick–slow pattern, the assumption was that this was a hidden chamber. The recorders were left running for twenty-four hours a day for a year – after which time the project was abandoned because the readings were wildly inconsistent. One day they suggested there might be a chamber in a certain place; the next day they revealed no such thing. The project had cost a million dollars and had taken a year – and for nothing. Disappointed, the Egyptian project-leader, Amr Gohed, said of the results: 'They are scientifically impossible. Call it what you will: occultism, the curse of the Pharaohs, magic – some force that defies the law of science is at work in the Pyramids.'

So, although the force is incomprehensible, we were still using our pyramids at Grange Farm, but in a different way. We are quite happy to use things empirically – and this also explains our circle. The circle, as a traditional symbol of perfection, represents eternity and completeness. We drew a double circle in white chalk on the bare floor of the lounge, where many of the disturbing effects had been felt. The family were involved in all of this, for that made, firstly, for a stronger belief system and secondly, it convinced them that we were doing something useful. Inside the circle we wrote a few magic words on the floor, the sort of words which have been used since time immemorial. While Rod was at one side of the circle writing *Ablanathanalba* (which is a word of protection based on Hebrew, Greek and Latin), Janice was on her knees opposite him chalking out *Tetragrammaton*, which is one of the secret names of God. I was at the side of them, writing *Elohim*, a biblical derivative which means 'the Divine Architect of the Universe' and *Agla*, which means something similar.

'Where do I put these?' asked Andy, coming into the darkened room carrying a hexagon and a pentagon – and we placed them at the appropriate points of the circle. To complete this traditional magical scene at Grange Farm, we all dressed up, covering our everyday clothes with black, monk-like robes. They have cowl hoods and tasselled belts around the waist. We lit a brass brazier of incense in the centre of the circle and scattered burning joss-sticks around the room. Eastern mystics believe that burning incense can enable one to reach between the plains of existence; that it can affect both this world and the world beyond. By the dim light of the brazier we lit candles, stood around the circle and chanted the appropriate words and phrases designed to dismiss our ghost.

Did we feel foolish – a bunch of professional people, scientists in the main, dressed in this way and taking part in the sort of ritual which many might dismiss as unscientific, superstitious mumbo-jumbo? The answer is, no, we did not feel at all silly saying and doing these things. There is no reason, just because one is a scientist, why one should be rigid and dogmatic. And if it works, why not use everything you can? We were using these traditional methods of magic for positive, not negative purposes. It is a psychological ritualistic method of influencing people's minds: our own minds, and those of the Hollands who were there with us, standing in the shady corners of the room behind us. If we were to get our collective unconscious into the right state, that would be quite enough to throw out unpleasant influences which emanated from the resident force.

We felt no dramatic effects as we performed our ritual. We reached the part of the ceremony where we said: 'Depart this place in the name of *Agla, Tetragrammaton*. Leave this place, whomsoever you may be,' and the candles seemed to flicker, giving out an elongated glow, but whether that was imagination or not, we'll never know. We could hardly see Sandra and her family in the darkened room and there was no evidence of paranormal phenomena such as might occur with an exorcism – vibrations, movements of objects, noises and so on. But as our two-hour procedure came to an end, the oppressive atmosphere lifted in that house. Sandra felt better immediately. She felt more in control – and so did everybody. Rod went upstairs again and returned looking happier than the last time he had climbed the stairs. 'It's fine,' he said. 'It's just fine.'

In the car on the way home, we were euphoric. It had gone well, but why had it worked? At this point, I have to hold up my hands and confess that it is beyond my scientific knowledge – beyond *everyone's* scientific knowledge – to offer hard-and-fast explanations. We threw all we had at the strange forces causing a disturbance at that house – and we succeeded. It had been important for the Hollands to be there with us, believing in us. To illustrate the suggestion behind this, I might refer to the strange case of the curing of a boy suffering from 'crocodile skin' (icthyosis). This is a debilitating condition in which the skin forms scales, becomes brittle and breaks easily, causing suppuration and infection. There is no effective treatment for the condition, and sufferers usually die as a result of the repeated infections they contract.

Dr Albert Mason was aware of the difficulties of treatment but arranged to hypnotize the boy. Aware that sceptics would try to attribute any potential cure to causes other than hypnosis – such as spontaneous remission – he suggested to the hypnotized child that the 'crocodile skin' should disappear from one arm only. The hypnosis worked and a jubilant Mason went on to clear up ninety per cent of the affected areas of the boy's body in the same way. Dr Mason's superior, a plastic surgeon called Sir Archibald McKindo, was astonished. 'You have performed the impossible!' he declared. Dr Mason then tried to cure another eight patients of the same condition. He failed dismally. Why? What was different about the healing of the boy and the healing of his subsequent patients? What had happened in between?

What had happened was that he had been told that what he had done was impossible. He 'knew' he could not do it, therefore he could not. It was not the boy's mind which cured his condition, but Mason's. Similarly, in India, doctors have given servants of seriously ill – even comatose – men 'medicine' that they, the servants, must take. The medicine is, in fact, a placebo, but the servants are told that the medicine is so powerful that if they take it, their masters will recover. The servants are so convinced of the 'medicine's' efficacy that it works.

We *thought* we could exorcize Grange Farm – and we did. More importantly, the Hollands thought we could do it, too. This is not auto-suggestion, because that is like implying that the Hollands brought the effects on themselves; that the boy with icthyosis brought it on himself. As we stood there after the ceremony, it was as if a heavy mist had cleared away from the house. The mind can do very weird things. Was it suggestion? Could the Hollands really have produced that 'mist'? And then could they have got rid of it? Who honestly knows? Whatever the force was, it had a final fling at Grange Farm. Within the next week, Roland Holland developed a seriously infected throat, my son Andy fell off a log and broke his leg and Sandra Holland was diagnosed as having cancer. Now, after treatment, she has been cleared and the Holland family are living in Grange Farm with no problems at all.

I can only conclude that there must have been a paranormal presence within that secret staircase. Had the culprit been the crossing of ley lines or cosmic rays, we might have achieved a temporary effect, but the disturbances would probably have returned. We experimented by using all the methods at our disposal. After all, when you go into an uncharted jungle, you take with you everything you can.

And there is no jungle more uncharted than the field of the paranormal, where Ghostbusters must tread with care!

2

Nolavar, the Golden Man and Associated Thought-Forms

The two young girls sitting opposite me in my study appeared a little uncomfortable – but not as nervous and upset as I had expected them to look. Usually, the suspicion that one is possessed by the Devil tends to destroy the Joe Cool in all of us! But Charlotte and Susan seemed relatively calm, if a bit withdrawn. I was impressed favourably with them. They were far from being little giggling unsophisticated schoolgirls, although this should not have surprised me: my teacher friend had said as much when he asked me to see them. 'These are bright, intelligent girls,' said Stanley when he rang. 'They're ex-pupils and because their families are away so much, I feel I want to help them. It seems they've got themselves mixed up with some sort of black magic – and I don't know anything about magic – black, white, pink or any other colour.' My ears instantly pricked up. There are few things more fascinating than magic. 'They're reluctant to discuss the matter with their parents,' continued Stanley, 'partly because they don't have close relationships with their parents and partly because the trouble involves certain boyfriends of whom the parents don't approve. Also the mother of one of the girls is an invalid with a weak heart. It's a Christian household, and she'd be upset to think that they had been involved with

27

anything mystical or a cult. The shock could kill her. You're the only person I could think of calling.'

The girls turned up the day after the phone conversation, arriving in Charlotte's car. At nineteen, she was at university. Susan was still at school, studying for her A-levels. They had an air of worldliness and considerable elegance, which took me by surprise. They were both pretty girls with long, straight, fair hair and were well-dressed in smart blouses and the uniform of youth, denim jeans. They sat back with deliberate composure, but I could tell that beneath this calm exterior they were quite tense. Almost as soon as they were seated, Charlotte lit the first cigarette of many. 'Start at the beginning,' I told them. 'And go on until you reach the end – and then stop.'

Susan smiled warily, looked at Charlotte and began. 'Charlotte was at my boarding school and I suppose the trouble all started when we went to visit some friends of my parents in the country. They had a very large old house, a manor house. Their children took us on a tour of the house and it was all great fun. There were wide corridors and staircases – the sort of house that the Famous Five might explore! Then they took us down into the cellars. Centuries ago they had been dungeons and they were horrible – smelly and dark. It was awful down there. I began to feel really peculiar.'

'She suddenly became very pale,' Charlotte added, 'and after that – even when we had returned home to our own houses – we had this awful feeling that something was with us all the time.' They tried to shrug off these unpleasant feelings, but the thing became more and more oppressive. 'It's hard to explain the feeling,' they said. 'It's just a presence.' Now, one of the things that a researcher comes across in possession is a sense of presence. During an exorcism, the presence, if it is really a possessing presence, will start by pretending it isn't there. It goes through stages, known as Presence, Pretence, Breakpoint, Voice, Clash and Expulsion. I shall explain more about these terms in a later chapter. Suffice it to say that I understood all too well what Charlotte meant by a sense of presence.

'The feeling became so strong that it seemed to pass from Susan to me,' Charlotte continued. 'Even when we weren't together, it would make one of us feel odd while the other was fine; then it would leave one and pester the other. It was so definite that we began keeping notes,' she added, and pulled out a diary cataloguing the dates and times when strange feelings would occur. I glanced through the diary.

'I'm feeling odd,' one entry read: 'I feel OK tonight,' said another. Flipping through the pages, it seemed they were very assiduous about keeping these notes and, as they explained, when they compared their notes they saw to their amazement and horror that when one wrote: 'Today has been bad, but I feel OK now. It's 10.30 and I'm going to sleep,' the other one would have written: 'I've been all right today but now it's half-past ten at night and I'm feeling suddenly awful. I think the thing is here.' And vice versa. There was an instantaneous changeover. It seemed that the presence had a routine. If they ever slept together in the same bedroom, it became even stronger. When one of the girls went on holiday there was a temporary amelioration of the situation for her, but no sooner did she come home than it all started up again.

'What about boyfriends?' I asked and they exchanged glances.

'Yes, we've both got boyfriends and the funny thing is that it seems worse when we're with them,' Susan said. 'It's hard to explain, but sometimes … well, it sounds silly, but when all this started, the boyfriends we had at the time sometimes seemed like different people.'

Charlotte added, somewhat hurriedly: 'Normally, you see, whenever they' – another exchange of nervous glances – 'tried anything on with us, if you know what I mean, they'd take "no" for an answer. But when this presence was around, we felt more carried away, and we somehow couldn't resist. It was as if something else made us behave like that and our boyfriends seemed to us to be suddenly more violent. I don't mean they hit us or anything … it was more like suppressed violence and they were just harder to control.'

'It was as if we were paralysed and couldn't stop them – although it wasn't like that for long,' explained Susan. 'It was like a temporary paralysis – but it was frightening to feel out of control.'

Interestingly enough, this is not unknown. There is a well-known condition known as sleep paralysis, in which you may wake up in the morning and find yourself unable to move, even though you are quite awake. Many people become very frightened about this. Actually, sleep paralysis only lasts very briefly – a matter of seconds – but because you cannot move, you feel that 'something' has got you, that you're being held down, possessed. It isn't that: it's merely that you've become conscious that the motor-centres of the brain are not yet functional. It's rather like sitting on your leg and it going to sleep. Until the blood starts again and the nerves get it to move, your leg won't move. If you didn't know, and it had never happened to you in your life, you might think: 'My God, I have a paralysed leg!' – and be very frightened indeed. But when you know that it is nothing more than sleep paralysis and it will pass off shortly, then you are no longer frightened.

So, could whatever was upsetting the girls temporarily affect the functioning of the motor-centres of their brains? We don't know the full extent of the effects of entities, poltergeists or spirits – call them what you will – but that personal, unconscious impulses can affect the way our minds function is very clear. They can affect us in all sorts of ways, from making us have hallucinations to causing us to experience actual physically objective events. So many mysteries remain to be solved, therefore I didn't doubt it when the girls told me they had had these unpleasant effects. Charlotte and Susan were beginning to feel they

were involved in a frightening, what they considered to be
an other-worldly, reality. 'And then there was the black
magic,' said Susan.

'Black magic?' I asked.

'We haven't done anything bad,' said Charlotte quickly,
'but we have been dabbling. We thought that we could
find out what was wrong with us by trying out a ouija
board, but that didn't help at all. Then we saw a medium –
and that did no good either.' So this was what they
thought of as black magic!

'I really don't think you need worry too much about
mediums and ouija boards and suchlike,' I advised, but
Susan quickly interjected:

'But that's not all. Things came to a head when we went
to a Hallowe'en Ball at the local village hall where people
were dressed as witches or wizards. There was a prize at
the dance for the best-dressed witch and wizard, and we
met a crowd of "wizards" – they were boys from the local
RAF camp. Because it was Hallowe'en, we started talking
about witchcraft and the occult. One of them [whom I
shall call Ralph] said, "I'm particularly interested in the
occult. Why don't you come back to the camp and I'll tell
you what I know about it?" '

The girls went quite enthusiastically, had a few more
drinks and Ralph lost no time in informing them that he
was, in fact, a Satanist himself. 'He showed us a room
decorated with demonic symbols and pictures of the
Devil,' revealed Charlotte, lighting up another cigarette. 'It
really scared us and we left as soon as we could, but things
got even worse after that.' Now Charlotte and Susan no
longer felt that they were haunted by just a vague
immortal something, but that Beelzebub – the Devil
himself – was following them. It took them a few weeks
before they managed to disentangle themselves from the
attentions of this youthful Satanist. He, of course, was
encouraging them in the conviction that his Master – the
Devil – wanted them for himself, to join him in his
activities; 'whatever they were,' said Charlotte and I

explained that since Satanists were not famed for their celibacy, it doesn't take too many guesses to imagine that sex played an overwhelming part in Ralph's plans for the girls. They smiled weakly. 'We were like nervous wrecks,' Charlotte said. 'The thing would climb into bed with us and touch our bodies. I could feel it touch me on my breasts and in other private places. It was horrible – and it was still going from one to the other of us.'

'I had a new boyfriend and whenever we were together, the entity went mad,' said Susan. 'It was awful. We would shake and tremble and feel very weak. My boyfriend felt it too, and then when I actually fainted when I was with him, he decided he couldn't put up with it any more and we finished.'

So by now, neither girl had a boyfriend – and it may be that this is what the entity wanted: both girls for itself. It was obvious to Charlotte and Susan that they needed help, but who were they going to call? Their families weren't the sort of people who would understand or sympathize with the supernatural in any way; and if they had learnt the girls had been dabbling in the 'wicked' occult, as typified by ouija boards, they would have been mortified.

'We must start somewhere,' I said. 'How did you know that this chap was really a Satanist?'

'Well,' said Susan, 'he told us quite openly. He boasted about it.'

Charlotte added: 'He had pictures of the Devil all over the place and cuttings from magazines on the same theme – pictures of Satanic ceremonies with nude women on altars and that sort of thing.'

'How old was he?'

'Probably about twenty-three or twenty-four,' they replied.

I told them that although he might have been a very funny fellow, he was not what could really be called a Satanist proper in any way, for he was far too young. From the picture that the girls painted of Ralph, I knew that he was just a young man who was excited by the idea of Satanism, black magic, naked ceremonies and so on. To have been a real Satanist, a student of the black arts hoping to acquire energies and powers from his infernal master, the Devil himself, he would have to have been very learned to begin with. He would have had to study various languages. And probably most importantly, he would not advertise the fact. The true Satanist will never talk openly to strangers, as Ralph had done. True Satanists stay very well hidden and they are usually pretty powerful people.

So, I told Charlotte and Susan, they were not being possessed by the Devil, summoned by Ralph. The girls were beginning to relax by now. Charlotte leaned back and lit another cigarette. Sheila, my wife, brought in cups of tea and the girls sipped, listening to what I had to say with an air of curiosity. They were so sensible that I thought I could easily sort them out. I would explain to them that their imaginations had run away with them, because my attitude is that while I'm very interested in finding psychical effects, I would first rather look for, and find, some rational psychological reason if people are upset. But it wasn't to be. For the paranormal force chose this very moment to manifest itself.

How do you describe an invisible presence? The prickling feeling on the back of your neck? The sense of not being quite alone? You can't see it, hear it, feel it – not in an accepted sense, at least. You can't even smell it. But you know that it's there, as surely as you see your friend standing next to you. You become so intensely aware of the presence that it can make the hair on the back of your neck and on your arms stand up on end. It can make your heart beat faster, make your breathing uneven. You may become dizzy. They are all effects which are most disconcerting, but we've no appropriate terminology to describe it so the description of the experience has to be an analogous approximation: you *sense* it, with a sense that isn't one of the five senses. And I could feel the entity at this point. I was studying it and I knew that it was studying me. I felt a total gut-reaction, like a magnet pulling at my insides.

It was testing me to see if I would be nervous, to see if I could be drawn into its sphere of influence. Maybe there was a certain telepathy involved, for there was no verbal communication. But neither was there anything running through my mind.

So the presence was there and in view of the information that Susan had given me – that she had been the first of the girls to become psychically aware of the entity – I decided that maybe it was an energy-form emanating from Susan herself, rather than an external, self-contained entity, which actually existed. Maybe. My theory went as follows: the girls had gone into the cellar of the house which was formerly a dungeon. They were sensitive, caring girls and I hypothesized that they would have been, like many other people, emotionally disturbed when the reality and horror of a dungeon struck them for the first time. We all read about dungeons in old castles and prisons as children, but we don't take into account the revulsion we can feel when entering a black, dank, subterranean place and realizing that in the past people have been chained up there, possibly for years. It is horrifying in the extreme. If you have ever been locked up – only for a few hours – you will know it's not nice.

The girls were intelligent. They knew all about ideas of spirits and entities existing, so what would be more likely than that, consciously or unconsciously, Susan or both of them would have had the idea that when they felt weak and dizzy down there (which could have been purely because of the physical effects of being low down, dark, underground, worried, nervous) they would think, my goodness, it must be the spirit, the ghost or the entity of somebody who died – and died most horribly down here, frustrated and lonely – which is haunting us? Maybe, I thought, Susan had inadvertently created a form of energy centring on a dead prisoner from the dungeon. I began to formulate a plan to deal with this extra, psychic personality. The girls were extraordinarily sensitive to this personality and were now showing some signs of being affected by it, becoming nervous and edgy – and I was feeling the sense of presence very strongly. I had a plan to exorcize this unwanted guest, but I certainly did not believe that it was necessarily something – a ghost or spirit of someone – which had existed in the dungeons. But the crucial thing was that the girls thought it was. They had created a thought-form.

Anyone working in the field of parapsychology will acknowledge the importance of thought-forms. They might be the lynchpin in hypothesizing about the paranormal. Carl Gustav Jung considered the possibility of thought-forms developing a 'life' of their own and in ritual magic and traditional voodoo, thought-forms are made much of. A thought-form is essentially a thought which after a given time, instead of just being a personal, subjective impression, becomes an objective form of energy that seems to exist in its own right. 'Thought-forms can be produced deliberately or accidentally,' I told Charlotte and Susan, who listened intently as I told them about the famous, amazing Philip experiment.

The Philip Group produced a spirit that had never existed. The group was based in Toronto and led by Dr George Owen, an ex-Cambridge professor of mathematics and genetics who had been involved with the Cambridge Psychical Research Society. He moved to Toronto to work in the department of preventative medicine and bio-statistics at the university – and he got together a group who held seances. It consisted of several housewives, a scientific researcher, an engineer, an accountant and an industrial designer – all sceptics. They weren't spiritualists or mediums; they were parapsychological investigators. That is, they were studying the phenomenon as scientifically as possible. Granted, there was an overlap between what you might do 'scientifically' and what could be achieved from the point of view of a spiritualist, but they were scientific enquirers without any pre-existing beliefs. They got together to see if they could tap tables by psychokinesis – the power to influence physical objects by sheer strength of will. They were, apparently, very successful either at contacting forces which could be viewed as being discarnate ('without a body') or, as some people might believe, at tapping energies from themselves. One day they decided, just as a bit of fun, to try to create their own fictitious spirit. (At that stage they thought of it as a spirit rather than as a thought-form.)

As part of this game, they made up a story about the spirit which they were going to 'contact'. They called him Philip. They gave him a history. They wrote it out. There is even a sketch in existence of Philip because one of the team drew a picture of him. Philip, they decided, came from a stately home in England called Diddington Manor – based on Diddington Hall in Warwickshire. Philip was a nobleman living in the early seventeenth century, who had a rather cold and frosty wife called Dorothea. He fell in love with a gypsy girl – Margo. When the wife found out about the affair, she was seized with jealousy and she accused Margo of being a witch. The girl was burned at the stake. Philip, because of his nervousness, did not intervene and he failed to save her. Subsequently he was so overcome with remorse, guilt and despair that he committed suicide by flinging himself off the battlements at Diddington Manor. This was, remember, total fiction – Gothic melodrama at its best – and they made it up as they went along; and since it took a year before anything happened, the story was embroidered more and more.

The group tried to contact Philip. 'Come on Philip, speak to us,' they said at seances – and of course, nothing happened. Did they really expect something to happen? Can people invent someone who doesn't – and has never – existed? You may well ask. But they kept on doing this regularly, among their other experiments, over the next year. They were about to give up and then they said:

'There's some information from other groups who are doing similar research that we're being too serious. Instead of sitting here po-faced and concentrating, let's talk and chat and become more relaxed and comfortable.' Strangely, paranormal events often occur when the experimental subjects relax. And suddenly, to their amazement, there was a bang on the table and it began to move of its own accord.

'Who is it?' they asked. 'One rap for yes, two raps for no. Is that Philip?'

Bang! It rapped once. 'Yes!' Good Lord!

'Who are you? Where did you live? How did you die?' they asked and they received their communications from Philip via raps. (In seances, words can be spelt out by calling out the letters of the alphabet: the 'spirit' raps at the appropriate letter.) Philip then told them the details they had made up. Then he increased the details. At one point he claimed that he was not in love with Margo, but merely sexually infatuated with her. He would make the table levitate all around the room and as each of the researchers, though colleagues, harboured quite natural suspicions that one of the others was faking, they took many precautions to prevent fraud. Often the raps on the table would take place in good light and the effects even occurred before the television cameras. Many people tried to detect fraud, but met with failure. Philip could be mischievous sometimes: he would not answer, or he would bang loudly or upset the table. He would even chase people with the table. On such occasions, the team threatened him; they would say, 'Look, if you don't stop misbehaving, we will dissolve you away. We brought you into existence and we'll un-invent you.' When they said this they would have quite a job bringing him back again. The raps would become faint and it took a lot of concentration for Philip to regain full power again.

Now we could call Philip, broadly speaking, a thought-form. Once you've brought a thought-form into existence, it then has a certain autonomy. It is not chained to its creator. This is the basis, perhaps, of ancient biblical stories – usually viewed as myths – such as that of the Golem, a product of ancient Hebrew mysticism. This may have been the first thought-form that was ever written about. The Golem was an artificial human moulded out of the clay of the earth by a holy rabbi, who would make it work for him in the house. He would construct a man out of clay and write one of the names of God – for instance '*Elohim*' – on the forehead of the Golem. The Golem was very efficient in the house. It had no mind of its own and had to do precisely what it was told. It was also tremendously strong. However, there is always a problem, of course. The story goes that as time passed, the Golem grew gradually more and more powerful. In the end, there would come a day when it would become unsafe and you had to get rid of it. There was only one way to do it, and that was by removing the word 'God' from its forehead. The rabbi would do this by rubbing out the equivalent of the letter 'E' from its forehead. One Golem, according to the myth, got out of hand on one occasion and managed to smash up a house before they rubbed out the name from its head.

We are going back here to mythology, to early biblical times. But there are further stories in later years, such as the relatively modern type of Golem, a creature of the mind, called in Tibet a *tulpa*. It is usually produced by a skilled magician and can be either human, animal or supernatural. One *tulpa* was created by the Hon. Alexandra David-Neel who was an explorer in the late 1920s and early 1930s. She spent fourteen years in Tibet, studying Tantric Buddhism with a number of lamas, thus becoming the only female lama at that time, which made her much revered. In her book, *Magic and Mystery in Tibet*, she explains how she was shown how to create an artificial human being: a *tulpa*. The story goes that it took her six months to create her thought-form of a holy monk, who was short, fat and jolly. This 'guest' stayed in her apartment and when she subsequently toured the country, the *tulpa* accompanied her, becoming so real and vivid that certain people visiting her in her tent would bow to the holy man in the corner, taking him for a real human being. David-Neel eventually found herself plagued by her *tulpa*. From being a jolly fellow, it began to look sly and malicious and escape from the control of its creator. Her nerves became worse and she described it as her 'day-nightmare', so she decided to dissolve it. This was not as easy as she might have planned: it took six months 'of hard struggle' – for the thought-form was 'tenacious of life'.

How, you may ask, are thought-forms created? Consider that the brain is a complicated mechanism and we use only twenty-five per cent of it. We have about seventy-five per cent unused. It is not beyond the realms of possibility that people with extraordinary powers of, for instance, telepathy or psychokinesis, are using the part of the brain unused by the rest of us – and it is this part of the brain of which we are unaware, that could well be responsible for creating all these strange effects. The Philip Group intended to make a spirit. They didn't know how, but this was their *intention* and the *intent* becomes the thing that makes it work. You cannot make the creation of a thought-form work by, as it were, grabbing hold of it in a physical way, by picturing the thing you want to create, whether a man or a monkey, and then by saying: 'Be like I'm thinking', but you do have to *intend* it to exist. That *intent* on your part seems to involve developing an aspect of your mind which is not under conscious control – the unconscious. We can contact the unconscious, but we cannot precisely control it. But if you *intend* it to do something – and you get it right – your intent will show that aspect of your mind what you want to happen. And if you are fortunate enough, it will then happen in conjunction with your desire. Artificially, people will do it with magic.

What this means is that if you believe, you can do nearly anything. Although I am not a believer in any religion, interestingly, in the Gospel according to Mark, Jesus urged his disciples to have faith, and said: 'What things soever ye desire, when ye pray, believe that ye receive them and ye shall have them.' *Believe* in me, he said, and you'll be cured. *Believe* and you'll go to heaven. The biblical authorities interpret this as meaning, for a start, that you must be a good person, and secondly that if you believe in Christ, then Christ will allow the wonderful power to work for you. But the point is not that. The point is that if you *believe* it will work, then it will – because of the powers within *you*, not within Jesus. When Uri Geller looks out of the television set and tells people: 'I will make your metal bend and your broken watches work; just look into my eyes', and your spoons are bent when you turn round, people think Geller must be fantastically powerful. What they do not realize is that it is *they* who are bending the metal, not Geller.

I believe there is an entirely logical reason yet to be found for thought-forms which come in all shapes and sizes. The thought-form, however, is different from a ghost *per se*, which takes on the form, appearance and motivation of a once-living person. It is a subtle distinction, rather like trying to explain to someone from a planet where a human being has never been seen, what the difference is between a real human, a model in a waxworks, a moving picture on a television screen, a hologram and a humanoid robot. He cannot understand the difference because to this visitor from another planet, all these examples of humans look the same. Sometimes they are similar, but we know they are not quite the same. In exactly this way, a thought-form and a ghost are not the same thing. They have different abilities.

Only a few weeks before Susan and Charlotte came to see me, I had been called out to an extraordinary case in Grimsby which bore some similarity to theirs, not least because it involved young women – a group of students who lived in a flat over the top of a dress shop. Janice and I went along to meet Elaine Lewis, a friend of one of my students, who had called us in, and her two flat-mates,

Helen and Jo. The flat is in an old, terraced group of houses and we reached it via a narrow passage which takes you to the rear of the building; a dark, Dickensian passage with a curving brick roof which forms the floor of the first floor above. The walls were damp and smelled of mould. This was certainly not Buckingham Palace. Elaine opened the door and we followed her up the rickety stairs to the flat, past a door which, she explained, was an unlit cellar, used for storing junk.

We could feel the bumpy floor beneath the carpet under our feet. The flat was a typical student flat. In other words, it was a mess. Elaine showed us into their sitting room where the other girls were, and we shivered. It was freezing cold and I kept my coat on. 'You see,' Elaine said, clearly knowledgeable about ghosts, 'there are cold spots.' I smiled. Actually, it didn't surprise me a bit that we were all frozen, because the room was huge and there was only a small electric fire at one end to heat it. Nothing supernatural there. There were posters all over the walls – everything from Che Guevara to lions and tigers – and a bed at one side of the room. Everything was higgledy-piggledy and untidy, but they were very pleasant girls. They made us some strong coffee which we tried to drink.

Elaine, a chubby blonde girl with pale grey eyes and freckles, was dressed in rather unbecoming, too-tight jeans. She had, I knew, had some unfortunate experiences with members of the opposite sex in her life – and I gathered that she had rejected men to such an extent that she wasn't really concerned about presenting a feminine image and, at least for the time being, preferred girls to men. As I talked to them, it struck me that the other girls thought in a similar vein. Could this have any bearing on the haunting? Maybe. Very often, emotional problems are associated with paranormal happenings.

'The haunting started when I was in the bath,' said Jo. 'I heard someone walk across the landing and knock on the bathroom door, but when I asked who it was, no one answered.' Jo had put on her bathrobe and went to the door, opened it. Nobody there. There was no one else in the flat. Later she asked the other girls if they had been playing a trick on her. They did not know what she was talking about. On the next occasion, Jo and Helen were in bed upstairs and Helen saw a figure standing next to Jo's bed. After that, Jo and one of her friends could hear someone in the living room when the room was empty. All the girls heard footsteps on their stairs and landing. Bangs were heard on the floor. Records were found melted and distorted, dolls were discovered, torn up. Then they each lost items of jewellery which turned up together on the mantelpiece. This is something which happens in many poltergeist cases. Poltergeists, in truth, are fairly boring and predictable creatures which do the same things. People who are afflicted with a poltergeist for the first time don't realize this, but when you're an investigator, you find it very samey. Often people will tell us what's happened and we think, oh, we know all about that. Let's hear something new!

One day, Jo thought she heard Helen calling to her and no one was in the flat. It seemed they had a ghost that could mimic the voices of the other occupants of the flat. That's more unusual. But then, the most astounding thing of all happened. 'I was walking past the cellar door one day and something made me turn and look in,' said Helen. 'There was a man standing there. But he wasn't an ordinary man. He was golden-yellow and glowing. He just stood in the doorway of the cellar until he eventually disappeared. I was struck dumb and I just couldn't move, I was so shocked. It was an elderly man with kind eyes – and he spoke to me. He said, "Have you got ..." but I couldn't hear the last word. It is always indistinguishable.'

'Always?' I queried.

'Yes, I've heard the voice several times since then. Sometimes I think I'm going crazy.'

The girls had felt a figure come into the room and sit in a chair. Jo came back to the flat one day, put the key in the door, felt it was icy cold and would not go in. Finally all three girls went in together. 'There was a strange smell in the sitting room – of burning meat, or meat that was slightly off,' said Elaine. 'And the cellar door was hanging wide open. The window was open.' Exactly a week later, they said, the same thing happened again, in precisely the same way. Then Jo was in the bedroom when she, too, saw the Golden Man – this time he was young – at close quarters.

'He came through the door, and was about two feet away,' she said. 'I always feel bad in the passageway between the front door and the stairs, but it was a real shock when I saw this man in the bedroom.' Then the girls discovered that one of the women who worked in the shop below their flat had been in the back yard one day with her small daughter and they had both seen a golden-yellow figure with staring eyes looking out of the flat window.

What did all this mean? Research showed that the houses were built over a graveyard and it was also discovered that several murders had taken place down the years on or around this site, when this part of the town was made up of little cottages belonging to fishermen. Grimsby was once a very rough and tough fishing port – and it is still one of the most violent small towns in the country. This district where the cottages had been contained a history of much trouble and perturbation. Add to that the graveyard, and you have considerable energies gathered in this place.

'We called in a medium and had a seance here,' said Jo. 'She told us that an old man had murdered his family with a spade in that very house after going mad. Then he hanged himself. And I met another woman who has never been in the flat but told me she had vivid, recurring dreams about it. She described the flat in detail, even though she has never seen it, and said that she dreamed that murders had taken place in the cellar. That's why it's so creepy down there.' Yet despite all the horror stories, when we asked them, none of the girls said they felt threatened by their Golden Man.

Janice and I went down to the cellar. It was very dark, damp, and dingy with a few sticks of furniture in it. There was certainly a most oppressive and weird atmosphere, but I had a suspicion that this was not a ghost. We returned to the flat a day or two later and put the Roboghost to work, getting violent blips at the cellar door and temperature changes on the landing which were very noticeable. After only a few minutes in every room, the sensor picked up violent changes of temperature, but not always going down; sometimes it went up. The girls told us that they were planning to leave the flat shortly, so it was ultimately decided that there was no point in taking any action. The fact was that no one had been hurt, simply that sensitive people had seen things. The flat was cold and draughty. A writer once pointed out that the electric light saw the demise of the ghost and it's true that if you like warmth and comfort, you get far fewer ghosts. Your sensitivities close down. Very often, it isn't necessary to do anything in such a case, but there were options open to us. We could have had a seance and contacted the 'ghosts' to tell them it was time for them to move on. If they refused, we could have had another seance and been a bit more threatening. It's no use being nervous about these things. You try to be as polite as possible. You don't threaten at first, but you don't whine either. However, I was convinced that this was not a ghost, but that rather it was another thought-form case. My reasoning was based on the form of the 'ghost'. It's very unusual, to say the least, to have a Golden Man ghost. Why did it take the form of a Golden Man? I think if we search deeply enough, we may find some answers.

Consider the evidence. The building is on the site of an old graveyard. There are various paranormal effects being produced there anyway. The flat was inhabited by three or four highly imaginative girls. They had already had experience with spiritualists. They were interested in magic and mystery, although this was the first time anything had happened to them. Nothing nasty occurred, but it was frightening. So there were many energies and forces around them. I think it would be clearly shown if you were to analyse the girls in depth – which it wasn't possible to do – that they would have some archetypal images in their minds of what they would assume a not-unpleasant haunting to be. Why a Golden Man? Early on, it had struck me very forcibly, you remember, that Elaine and indeed the others, were into female companionship in quite a heavy way, but I believed that they still liked men. Well, I think the mind will produce things in conformity to one's expectations to a great degree, and although they didn't consciously expect to see a Golden Man, it's not too far to stretch the imagination to see that this would be a vivid, non-sexual entity that was essentially male, but innocuous and non-threatening.

They were not religious, so they would not see a Jesus figure. What was the next best thing? Could it not be the Golden Man; golden like an angel? Although it was male, it wasn't emasculated, but it was innocuous. Not threatening, but comforting. Not exactly a father figure, but not a man who would want to take advantage of them. It was a thought-form. They had created it. But there were powerful energies already in that place. They may have created their Golden Man out of a substance which already existed, in the same way that you would mould a new figure out of Plasticine. The Plasticine was already there: it might have been in one particular shape before they started to play with it and re-form it, but it was still the same basic substance. The girls just made it appear differently. I think that perhaps in many 'paranormal' sightings, people do just that. They utilize the pre-existing matrix that is there and mould it to conform to what the conscious or unconscious mind wants to produce.

Don't forget that you are not always consciously aware of what you want to do, but it still happens. It is well known in psychology that people act in a particular way and say: 'Why did I do that? I didn't want to do that', but something in them was driving them to do it. In my view, the Golden Man was probably a thought-form created by the repressed energies of the girls in the flat, in conjunction with the matrix of energy which was already there. Usually, almost inevitably, we do not find a haunting where there are no people around. This may sound like a Catch 22 situation: if there's nobody there, how do you know if there's anything going on or not? But you can leave monitors in a place and discover that nothing much seems to happen until there are people there whose energies have to be involved with it. We can then hypothesize: does '*it*' use a person's energies, or does the *unconscious mind* of the person become sufficiently infused with the energies and create the performance, to the surprise of the person, who doesn't realize they are doing it?

Why should the unconscious do something that we don't know about? Does that seem rational? It's perfectly rational, actually. For example, we might have a very frightening dream and wake with our hearts pounding, breathing level raised, blood pressure up. We have no control over our dreams. We see this effect during sleep, but that part of the mind, given free rein in a haunted house, may act in this way when we are awake. (Is there any difference between being awake or asleep as far as the unconscious is concerned? Probably not.) We are not *intending* to produce a frightening effect but part of our essential make-up *is* producing it.

One of the primary abilities of Charlotte and Susan's sinister thought-form was clearly menace. It was there in my study, darkly menacing the girls and doing its damnedest to menace me as well. The thought-form and I were engaged in a mystical battle. I deliberately let the entity continue to manifest for a while because I wanted to study it and observe, particularly, its effect upon the girls, who were getting more and more jumpy. Susan grasped Charlotte's wrist and they looked at me with panic. I just watched, probably making them more nervous with my steady gaze, but my concentration was elsewhere. I finally decided that I did not want the entity there any longer – so

I attacked it. I produced another entity: an entity that was bigger, nastier, more powerful than the one bothering the girls – and more importantly, it was on our side. And it didn't want the other entity there. I produced Nolavar.

How did I do it? You will recall that Dr Owen's psychic research group conjured up a 'spirit' called Philip whom they had invented. For some time previous to meeting the girls, I had been experimenting at producing a similar thought-form, an entity. Most convenient, as it turned out, for I had managed it: my very own *tulpa*. My entity's name was Nolavar. The name was a bit of fun, really. You can have any name you want, but if you take the 'r' off, he's very mystical: 'Avalon', spelt backwards, which is where King Arthur came from. There were very powerful magicians around in those days! I pictured Nolavar as a huge and very powerful entity, a vast, semi-amorphous life-form. Nolavar is not a human form at all, not a male or female, but an 'it' – and extremely alien. I did not want a human form on the grounds that there were enough of those around anyway. I fancied something different. I pictured Nolavar as arriving from some distant region in another dimension. Nolavar is like an amoeba, with pseudopodia – legs and arms – when he needs them. Because he is a thought-form and amorphous, that means he can be big, small, nowhere or everywhere. Potentially, he can go through the eye of a needle or engulf a whole city.

Curiously, other people at seances I have attended have felt Nolavar's presence, whether he is happy, whether he is not; whether he is in fine fettle or ill-humour. Sometimes when we feel that he is there, he will produce effects. He may rap, tap or maybe move a small ornament. Nolavar communicates with raps on the table and says: 'Yes, this is Nolavar,' rather like Philip did. You may say, and quite rightly, that surely if you believe it will work, it will work. I agree and if it works I am quite happy. He has never appeared, visibly. But the sense of his presence is undeniable. And, as the experiences of Charlotte and

Susan had shown, the sense of presence is a very real thing. Nolavar can be as present as that.

Gradually my experiments were showing that Nolavar was developing an existence of his – or its – own. I'm not saying that Nolavar could necessarily stop a car that was in full flight towards me or something of that nature. But he was handy. It was like having one's own god-form. Nolavar seemed to be very helpful in many ways. I had constructed him deliberately so that he could, if the necessity arose, exert considerable power. Now came the opportunity to test the effectiveness of my experiment and the efficiency of my thought-form. I called upon Nolavar to clobber the entity which the girls had conjured up or were being bothered by, whichever one it was. I knew that unless the entity was very powerful and very persistent indeed, it would not be able to withstand the force of my pre-existing thought-form. The girls, however, did not need to know about or believe in Nolavar and Charlotte and Susan had no idea of my plan. I just looked at them and I 'called' Nolavar inside my head. It worked like magic – which many people would claim it was. The effect was instantaneous. I received a strong impression that the girls' entity was terrified. The atmosphere cleared instantly and the girls' faces were a study. 'It's gone!' they both cried in chorus. 'It's gone!'

Interestingly enough, in the stories of people who have been disturbed by what are called night-time 'visitations' of succubi or incubi – which are sexual entities – a strange effect is that when the entities disappear they leave behind a curious emptiness. Again, we haven't the terminology to describe it. But if someone who has been in the same room with you, a friend or an enemy, leaves, whether you are pleased or sad that they have gone, there is a sense about the room which you expect and you are used to. But if your friend or enemy is one of these succubi or incubi, then when they have gone the feeling is curiously different. Your mind cannot grasp that they have ever been there at all. The atmosphere is so clear, so empty, that you become convinced – despite your positive, definite knowledge that you were 'experiencing' something – that nothing was ever there at all. There are many records of this utter blankness, this sense of non-existence, as if it's anti-matter: gone. This is what happened to Charlotte and Susan when whatever had been bothering them had been attacked by Nolavar. It absolutely and completely went, leaving a vacuum.

The question remained: what was it? Was it something that came from the unconscious of one of the girls? Had it gone back there? Was it something external to them that shot back to wherever it had come from? We can hypothesize for a long time. All that was certain was that they both exclaimed that it had gone. In some way it seemed that my mental construct of Nolavar existed in the same reality mode as the girls' tormentor, and if it did, then Nolavar won the day. Of course, I believe that the dungeon, the suggestibility of Susan, the observation by Charlotte and her other friends that Susan was 'not herself', were, under the circumstances, enough somehow to hypnotize her into a belief that something nasty had got hold of her. And she quickly produced, then, an image which drew sufficient energy from her to develop its own quasi-reality.

It is easy to dismiss these hypotheses as mere conjecture. But it must be remembered that the girls had no idea what I was thinking and they did not know what to expect – or what I expected. They could not have responded to non-verbal cues in my behaviour or subliminally observed ones, or, of course, even if they had observed them, subsequently acted in a way expected of them. I did not tell Susan and Charlotte there and then the truth of what I had done, because that would have given their conscious minds a chance to object. If I had explained it to the girls, they might have said to themselves: 'Well, that's what he *says* – but is it true? Is it really that?' You do not need to know what an antibiotic does when you take it. It just does its work at a level that you do not need to have anything to do with. The girls did not need to believe in Nolavar, but because *I* believe he exists, my plan worked. In this degree only, I would support religious ideas: if you believe in something strongly enough, it can perhaps help you in times of need, though not because it has an objective existence – because you are the one who has thought it into existence.

The existence of thought-forms is at best tenuous to us. In the climax to the first film of *Ghostbusters*, the devil-creature tells the Ghostbusters that he is going to appear in the guise of whatever comes into their minds. They try to keep their minds blank but he comes as a thought-form: the Staypuft Marshmallow Man, which one of the team foolishly allows to enter his mind. It was wonderfully entertaining as the giant Marshmallow Man crashed through the streets to do battle, but the concept is connected to the old Judaic idea that God should not be visualized as being anything. He should not be pictured as a venerable old man with a long white beard, sitting on a throne, any more than he should be pictured as a Marshmallow Man. Whatever enters your mind probably *IS*. That is the point with thought-forms.

The Owen Group produced Philip. Alexandra David-Neel claimed to have created a thought-form in Tibet and eventually got rid of it. I got rid of Charlotte and Susan's thought-form. Where did it go? Where did Philip go? Where did that piece of ice in your saucer go? It turned into water. Where did the water go? It evaporated. Where did it go? Where do all thought-forms go to? Do they remain real? If thought-forms remain real because of people's belief in them, then there must be a God. There would certainly be Jesus and Buddha; and probably more strongly still, there would be Osiris, Isis and Horus – Egyptian gods – because they were believed in for far longer than Christianity has been. If believing – concentrating on them for longer – makes them stronger, then we have got quite a number of massive archetypes somewhere hovering around. A theologian once remarked that if God didn't exist, it would have been necessary to create him – and I do feel that men create God in their image, rather than the other way round. If we were twelve-toed Martians with tentacles, then that is how our God would be depicted.

As far as Susan and Charlotte's thought-form was concerned, they remained free of their mutual obsession from that time on. Nolavar and I had fixed it.

3

Move Over, Doctor Van Helsing

The bright August sunshine glanced across the square Norman tower of Skidbrook church as we approached it along the winding country road. I was unfamiliar with this part of Lincolnshire, so Janice and I had a personal guide: Mark, a young man who had attended some of my lectures on the paranormal at a local college. His weird adventure at the church, in company with five other students, had brought us here, but looking at the pretty little church, I couldn't help but reflect that it appeared harmless enough, standing there, well back from the road, surrounded by tall trees and a yew hedge. We left the car at the gate and strolled up the long path to the disused church, with Mark leading the way. The sun was warm; the birds were chattering to each other in the trees and the smell of the lush summer foliage filled our nostrils. We had no clue that we were heading towards the most frightening experience of our lives.

The previous day I had received the phone call from Mark. He was a student of eighteen or nineteen, studying land surveying. As part of a college project on old buildings he and his fellow-students visited old churches and cathedrals. A group of six – three boys and three girls – had gone to Skidbrook in two cars and they had eventually fled in fear. Mark, although as scared as the rest of his friends that night, also had an academic interest in unexplained phenomena – and he knew that when he telephoned me he would find a ready ear. 'Perhaps you can tell me why people might be lighting fires in a circle around the church,' he suggested. 'And why there are dead birds with their heads cut off in the churchyard. Why are there burnt-out red and black candles inside a church which isn't used? Do you think there's a cult out there, or something?'

'I don't know,' I said. 'Let's go and look.'

The gargoyles beneath the roof grinned at us as we approached the church along its tree-lined drive. Instead of having ordinary drainpipes, Skidbrook has curved gargoyle faces at each corner of the roof guttering. The church has a forgotten feel to it. Certainly this is not a tourist spot worth looking at as a point of historical interest, unlike Lincoln Cathedral or even Louth church, which is not far away. Louth has one of the oldest churches in England with one of the highest spires, which is quite unusual because it's only a little church. But no one would go to Skidbrook for any reason at all. It is small, in an unknown village, miles from anywhere and no longer used. The old church is still consecrated, but the interior is completely empty; there is no altar, no pews. The grounds, however, are still kept more or less tidy although, as we were to discover as we strolled around, some of the tombstones on the graves had been disturbed.

'Those tombstones are really creepy,' Mark remarked, pointing to them. These were tombs which were raised about eighteen inches from the ground, covered with big stone slabs. Some of the slabs had been moved sideways so you could look down into the cavities of the tombs. We walked across and peered in. 'You can't see much in there,' said Mark. 'It's just dark.' We wandered around the grounds, inspecting the charred remains of the fires about which Mark had spoken. Forming a circle about three to four feet in diameter around the church were half a dozen sites of fires. 'And look at these,' Mark said, pointing to the ground close to the church door. There were a few dead birds lying with their throats cut. They were apparently drained of blood. With one foot, I moved the small corpses to one side and we entered the church. It was pretty messy: totally empty, apart from an enormous tomb at the far end, and the door had either been broken open at some point, or merely left open, so it was not locked. A bit of wire hung off it. Perhaps the church had been broken into so often that the powers-that-be gave up locking the door. Inside, as Mark had said, red candles and black candles stood on the window-sills, burnt down. We had already spotted another candle on a window-ledge outside the church. 'Do you think it's black magic?' Mark asked as we left the church, pulled the heavy doors closed behind us and sat down on the step.

'Hmm, perhaps,' I replied, glancing around. Clearly something had been going on here and such a place could be very useful for some types of black-magic ritual. I do not include witchcraft in this, by the way, because witches are pagan and not interested in Christianity and Christian churches. Satanists, on the other hand, would be keen on using a church for certain perverse rituals, because they would enjoy reversing Christian things. So instead of having white candles, they would have black ones; instead of being kind to animals, they might chop them up in the churchyard. 'Tell Janice and me exactly what else happened when you came here with your friends,' I instructed Mark. I already knew the story, but Janice had not heard it first-hand.

Well, everything was all right here until it got towards evening. Then the girls started saying they didn't like the atmosphere. We asked why and they said there was something eerie about the place. Well, you know how interested I am in spooky things, so of course this made me all the more intent on staying. I said, 'Why don't we stay until it gets a bit darker and see what happens?' So we did. The girls weren't a bit keen, but we bullied them into it. They got more and more nervous as it got darker and eventually one of them – Kate – collapsed crying and saying she couldn't stand the atmosphere and wanted to leave. We were about to tease her about it, when we suddenly felt this horrible sort of atmosphere too. It was a strange oppressive feeling. Then as the sun went down, we could see mist coming from those open tombstones there.

Mark pointed, but the disturbed tombstones in that old-fashioned little churchyard surrounded by hedges (which appeared to have been shaped by a budding topiarist) looked innocent enough.

The mist became thicker and thicker and then we thought we saw two tall figures who looked as if they were wearing cloaks, moving through the bushes, silently. That really got to us. Each of us said, 'I don't believe this', but the atmosphere seemed very menacing and from being quite warm it suddenly went very cold. What finished us off was some peculiar little points of light which suddenly appeared in the mist. They were little, twinkling, golden spots that seemed to be coming towards us. Then they moved sideways. It was so scary. Kate looked as if she was about to faint and one of the other girls, Liz, was getting into a state. We decided to leave. It may have been imagination, but as we ran down the drive to the road where the cars were, these little twinkling points of light seemed to follow us in the mist, right past all the bushes. It was as if they were showing us the way out.

As they drove home, one of the girls couldn't stop crying and Mark admitted that he felt emotionally disturbed too. He couldn't understand the impulse he had to weep. The girl sobbed on the back seat, but when they asked her afterwards why she was crying, she said: 'I don't know.' As soon as they got away from the drive, she recovered. I think it's absolutely undeniable that women are more sensitive to such things than men. My friend Keith Hearne, who has written about premonitions and premonitory dreams, has shown statistically that more women than men have premonitions, and there's certainly a female bias as far as extra-sensory perception is concerned.

So now, Janice and I had seen the tombstones, the empty church, the burnt-out red candles and the remains of the fires. I could not tell Mark precisely what had gone on, but I could confirm that it was abnormal and I could guess that people who were involved with a cult of some form or another might take advantage of the fact that the church was still consecrated. A consecrated church can be 'damaged' in a spiritual or mystical sense, and this church could easily be attacked because there was nobody around to defend it: no police, no wardens – even though the grounds were still looked after to a degree. From a diabolical point of view, sacrilege agitates the existent forces on that site and offers a power-source. Remember also, that many old churches are built over pagan sites which were not chosen randomly. Our ancient forebears were often known to have ways of choosing sites for their pagan rituals that we are not able to understand, and many of them were built on the faults which are known as ley lines. So however the ancients did it, there may be forces of some sort at these particular points.

I wondered what had happened to the birds. They were desiccated, mummified, dried up, there was no blood in them at all, which is what you would expect to find if they were old corpses and maggot-ridden, but they seemed to have been drained of blood. We know there are barmy cults which go in for blood-drinking. Aleister Crowley, the famous old black magician, reports on Raoul Loveday, the poet, who died after drinking cat's blood at one of their ceremonies. I believe he died of enteritis – possibly feline enteritis! We decided to go back with the group and spend a night there, which was why, a few days later, we rolled up at Skidbrook in the mid-evening, well equipped with the Roboghost, the Tractron Beam, the Probe, some torches and even big Ben, our ghost-getting dog! The electrical equipment runs off batteries, which is why we need our big ghostmobile car. The limo has enough room to store two or three spare batteries, but it would be impossible to get all the equipment, the batteries, together with the dog and ourselves, in an ordinary car. The Tractron Beam is a boosted strobe light which was developed by my son Andy. We can mix certain colours into it, which has a powerful effect. It looks very much like the proton pack and proton wand which are used in the *Ghostbusters* film, with a grey metal tube held rather like a gun. It has a charger at one end and the bulbs are inside it. It runs off electricity or the batteries, which are kept in the back-pack. You simply press a button and the light-beam comes out – a very intense beam, emitted in bursts. It's much more dazzling than ordinary light and is most disconcerting. Light is very disagreeable to entities. Another talented member of the team, Rodney, developed the Roboghost and the Ion Detector, which is a life-field detector, and the Probe was developed by a former member, Steve Morley.

The Ion Detector is a small hand-held device which looks exactly like a remote control for a television set. If you bring it close to somebody, little green lights go on and off in sequence, depending on how strong the life-force is. The life-force is, basically, the electromagnetic radiation of living beings. We've had some small responses on this and it seems it might be very useful, but it does raise questions, such as would we receive responses from a life-form other than a living human being? The Russians have already invented something similar which they claim can respond to the 'bio-plasmic body' from three feet away, to detect what spiritualist mediums would call the aura, but although they developed it for parapsychological reasons, ghost-spotting was not among them.

As we set up our equipment inside the church, we were careful not to make too much noise or, as it became darker, show too much torchlight. It was about half an hour after midnight when we first noticed something odd. The Roboghost's 'voice' was not operative, but the monitors were showing responses in the seismic – that is the vibratory – and the light-intensity modes. Probe in hand, Rodney went in search of the source of the cause of this, while I continued to observe the monitors. The area near the door of the church seemed to be an active spot. Andrew quietly opened the door and peered into the darkness outside, where the only light came from the moon. Rodney looked over his shoulder. There came a deep growl from nearby: Ben, silent until now, had risen to his feet and, hackles up, stood motionless. Suddenly, Andrew closed the door and leaned his back against it.

'Did you see that?' he asked Rodney.

'The figures? Were they shadows?' replied Rodney. Janice and I drew close. 'They certainly didn't look solid,' he added. Was it imagination, fuelled by the reports of Mark, which had caused both Rodney and Andrew to believe they had seen two 'shadows' gliding silently across the path which led to the church? Or was something very strange going on?

'Janice, you stay and watch the machinery; we'll go and have a look around,' I said and, armed with torches, Ion Detector and Tractron Beam, the three of us stepped from the sanctuary of the church, out into the darkness.

'I'll wait here,' said Rodney, positioning himself close to the church door, his torch lighting up the archway. Andrew and I set off, Andrew holding Ben's lead. We had gone only a few steps when there was a scuffling noise just in front of our feet. 'What's that?' asked Andy, and shone the beam of the torch downwards. It was an unpleasant sight: a decapitated bird, like the ones Janice and I had observed on our first visit, apart from the fact that this one had obviously been killed very recently, lay bleeding from the neck.

'A newly killed bird,' I called over my shoulder to Rodney, and he made an expression of distaste. There was no sign of the bird's killer, but it seemed as though there was some very physical agency at work here rather than a paranormal one. At the time, that seemed to me to be the most frightening prospect. I thought, Oh God, there's going to be trouble here, believing that the group which was doing these things was somewhere around. After all, had not Andrew and Rodney seen someone outside? We did not want to get into a physical battle with any group. We did have Ben with us, and he is a big chap, and Andy's our hard man, so we could defend ourselves to a degree, depending on how many of them there were, but we really wanted to avoid a punch-up. Ben did not help us to feel calm as we stepped gingerly along. Growling ferociously, he tried to plunge off into the bushes and only with a struggle was Andrew able to hang on to him. In the moonlight we could see mist all around us. It felt wrong. Bad? Evil? What's the right word? My stomach turned.

'I'm feeling rather ropey,' I muttered to Andrew.

'It's so claustrophobic,' he whispered in reply. 'I don't know whether it's a trick of the darkness, but there seem to be moving shadows everywhere.'

'Imagination,' I retorted stoutly, but it was said with more confidence than I felt. The shadows seemed alive and they certainly looked ghostly. 'Bloody hell,' I murmured under my breath. I was torn between a desire to deal with these things which were ominous and threatening, and the urge to 'watch' them, as if I was a disembodied observer. For, undeniably, it was fascinating. I wanted to see what could possibly happen, bearing in mind that if it was going to be very powerful, could we cope? I suppose it's like asking: 'Why do you want to climb a mountain?' to which the answer is usually: 'Because it's there.' Why didn't we stop straightaway? Because we wanted to see what would happen! There was a cry from the church and we looked back.

'Rodney!' called Janice, 'The instruments are going wild! And it's freezing in here!'

'That's funny,' I heard Rodney say to her. 'I'm feeling so hot, I could be on fire.'

Andrew and I turned back to our path, but we felt suddenly disorientated and confused. There was mist everywhere and I felt a chill as I saw that a thicker, greenish-coloured mist was rising from the partially opened tops of the disturbed tombs which seemed to loom around us. It looked like smoke but this smoky stuff was nasty; it offered a feeling of decay and exuded something to make your stomach churn. What colour was it? What colour is slime? The fog had a green, cloying blackness. And how can something you see make you feel sick? For I was suddenly overcome by nausea. 'Let's get back to the church,' I said, perhaps a trifle nervously, and we tried to retrace our steps. There was no mistaking the sense of threat contained in the dense fog and I flicked the torch this way and that, but the beam was swallowed in the smoky mist. The oppressive feeling grew stronger and I took the Tractron Beam from Andy, prepared to use it if necessary. We groped our way back to the church. As Rodney came to meet us, he stepped on something soft. As he shone the torch-beam down, we saw it was the dead bird.

'I thought you said this bird had only just been killed,' he said as he bent to examine it. To our amazement, the bird, which had been bleeding copiously only minutes before, now appeared to be drained of blood. It was desiccated and almost mummified. This was something new – and the puzzling part was that even if there had been some kind of bloodthirsty cult group using the churchyard that night, how could they have achieved such a phenomenon as draining blood from a corpse within a few silent minutes, without Rodney, who was standing nearby, witnessing anything? Had Andrew and I simply *imagined* that the bird had been newly-killed and bleeding? Or could something even more terrifyingly supernatural be going on?

Most of the human 'vampires' – that is, murderers – whom we know about, have actually sucked blood from the necks of their victims. John George Haig would bite the neck of his victim and drink from it. Sometimes he would cut the neck and let the blood run into a cup and drink it. Fritz Haarmann actually bit out the throats of young boys to kill them. Now, here we were, in a graveyard at the dead of night with a blood-drained corpse at our feet and our imaginations inflamed beyond belief. Were we entering Bram Stoker territory? Was the story of Dracula more than just fiction? I found myself worriedly pondering this outlandish question as we sought the protection of the church with its sanctuary of light from the torches, away from the dark, oozing mist behind us. Thoughts of the Highgate vampire flicked across my mind. At Highgate Cemetery in London, ghost-sightings are frequent and there are claims that a real vampire emerges from a tomb and has attacked girls in his undead wandering. When one is in a cemetery at midnight surrounded by moving shadows, evil-looking fog and blood-drained corpses, believe me, it is not quite so easy to shrug off these tales as being fantasies as it is in the broad daylight! And there were inexplicable events at Highgate: for instance, when a crew from Thames Television went to film a 'vampire-hunter' at the cemetery, they set out in light-hearted mood, but although it was broad daylight, the evil atmosphere managed to spook them all. What is more, they were unable to film; a strange noise repeatedly interfered with the sound. Then the camera director fainted – and the programme had to be abandoned. As we entered the church and pushed the heavy doors closed, as if to emphasize my thoughts, Janice pointed upwards. 'Look: bats,' she said in a low voice. 'They seem awfully big.'

We aimed our torches upward and in the dim light we could see two bats swirling around inside the roof of the church. But what sort were they? I'm a bit of a bat fan, and have studied them. But these were like no bat I had ever seen. Certainly not the native pipistrelle bats, which are sweet little fellows, or the Natterer's bats. Something about these two made me shiver. They were huge, like the *Desmodus rotundus* – better known as the vampire bat – although these do not live in Britain. They are much bigger than our bats, with a wingspan of about a foot, and live only off blood because they cannot digest solid food. The vampire bat does not actually hurt its victim, it just kills it by mistake – for its teeth are so sharp that even if the bat did not have an anti-coagulant in its saliva to ensure that the blood continues to flow, animals would often bleed to death because the cut would not heal. The beasts often contract rabies, too, for the vampire bat is a carrier. And the animal may not even know it has been bitten. So these bats are very different from our ordinary bats, which eat insects. My mind whirled with wild horrors of vampires, stakes, bats and the undead. This is crazy, I thought, looking upwards. Get a grip. But I could not believe what I was seeing. We could hear a vague swirling sound in the air – not as loud as birds' wings, so these bats were not completely silent fellows – but it certainly made all of us wonder whether they were ordinary bats or not.

'Spooky,' said Andy, as if reading my mind. 'And I didn't even bring my cross and garlic.' The tension we were all feeling was eased for a moment.

'At least everything seems all right in here,' said Janice in a low voice. She spoke too soon, for with a tremendous crash, the double doors of the church were flung open and tendrils of the thick mist began to insinuate into the interior of the building.

'Ye gods!' breathed Rodney as the greenish, suffocating cloud began to swirl around us and we looked in mystified horror into the mist where, to our amazement, we could see points of light which seemed to swing eerily to and fro. The faint flapping noises from the bats were drowned in the noise of distant hissing which mounted to an ominous rumbling. My skin prickled with fear. I wondered if these points of light were what Mark and the others had seen. If so, no wonder they were frightened, for this was most peculiar. We, at least, had been a little prepared for such events, but the group of students had not been. The little lights, about the size and colour of the brass head of a drawing-pin, glittered oddly in the mist. Clearly there was no physical explanation. Had it been a human, holding some light-source, we would have been able to see his body, but these were like little golden stars of energy, moving around within the mist. We stood stock-still, the pressure on us growing. I felt as if I was developing a headache as the low rumbling noise persisted.

'Ugh!' cried Janice, her hand on the back of her neck. 'I'm sure I felt something touch me!'

Andy's hand tightened on the Tractron Beam and he swung around, aiming it into the mist. 'Will this be any use? Shall I fire?' he asked in a low voice, adding in confusion: 'And where shall I fire?'

'Hold on,' I replied, the pounding in my head increasing. 'Let's wait and see what happens.' We held our breath. The coldness was intensifying by the second, but suddenly the thick mist began to leave the church the way it came, swirling out of the doorway until the interior was completely clear. Watching it gush away, we exhaled with relief – then a loud crack from the far end of the church made us spin around. The burnt-out candles which had been standing on a ledge had fallen to the floor. They rolled a little way and then stopped. There was no wind, everywhere was motionless and there was a sense of expectation in the atmosphere. All four of us felt a telepathic force, an invisible presence which seemed to be waiting for our next decision. The open door beckoned.

'This is where you should go,' the invisible force seemed to be saying. 'Leave now. You'll be all right if you leave now.' We waited, immobile, not daring to so much as breathe in the darkness. 'If you don't go,' we felt the presence saying, 'you will suffer the consequences.'

The consequences rapidly made themselves felt. What I had taken to be my throbbing headache became clearly defined, as a dull thumping shook the building. Boom-boom, boom-boom. Louder and louder came the thuds, smothering us in sound. The noise was palpable. It invaded our senses. Breathing became harder and we looked at each other in anxiety. 'This is getting too weird for comfort,' said Rodney, pulling uncomfortably at the round neck of his summer sweater. From outside there came a gigantic crash and we were startled into action. Rushing to the door, we shone four torch-beams into the churchyard and gazed out. Someone – or something – had further dislodged one of the tombstone lids which we had previously noted to have been disturbed. The six-foot stone slab lay on the ground, split asunder.

'What could have done that?' gasped Janice and as if in answer there came a sound from behind us: a low growling. We turned quickly, but could see nothing, for the church, which only seconds ago had been clear of smoke, appeared to be filling up again, but this time the source of the blackish-green mist was the dark recesses of the building, from where the growling noise emanated. As the fog billowed towards us, the growling grew louder. We had reached the point where it was necessary to suspend disbelief quite completely. This was the most nerve-wracking experience we had ever encountered; this threatening sound was clearly engineered to get us away from the place. The odd thing about this fog was its definition: it was like a cloud, with a clearly-defined, swirling top, like the centre of a black cauliflower.

I confess, we were frightened. In the daylight, we may say we were not, but we were filled with that primeval fear: the fear of the unknown. We had no idea what was going to happen next – or whether we were equipped to cope with whatever was to come. As the cloud moved closer and the growling became louder, the risk became apparent: were we going to be engulfed and destroyed? This was the most fearsome foe we had come across and there was only one option left open to us: to use the Tractron Beam. But if that didn't work, what would we do then? Run, I suppose. 'Andy!' I shouted. 'Use the beam!'

He did not need telling a second time. With a flick, the Tractron was activated and an intense beam of light snaked into the green blackness of the fog. None of us knew exactly what to expect. For an awful moment I thought the beam would be swallowed up, but then all hell – literally – let loose. The pounding hit a crescendo and with a roar which made us think the church was falling down, the fog exploded, blinding us with the light of a myriad colours. The light of the Tractron Beam seemed to have been reflected off particles inside the cloud, back at us. We stood our ground as a shower of light and colour fell about us, Andy manfully holding the Tractron Beam steady. We shielded our eyes and as the roar faded away, we uncovered them to see that the mist had gone; the interior of the church was clear and silent, lit by our powerful beam. Andy swung the beam around. In the roof, bats were tossing to and fro; there were so many that it seemed as if all fifteen species of native British bat were flitting, startled at being momentarily captured in our powerful ray. But there was no sign of the two huge bats we had seen earlier. Quickly, Andy turned off the Tractron Beam.

Outside the church, we could hear the trees rustling gently in the intermittent breeze as we examined the inside of the building. 'Hey, look at this,' I called to the others. Beneath one of the windows at the far end of the church was an empty tomb, like a big stone coffin with a solid lid. The lid had shattered into a thousand pieces. If the energy, or whatever it was, had been contained in that tomb, the effect of our violent response must have resulted in this. There was such power here, we pondered. If somebody had not had instrumentation as we had – the Tractron Beam – I don't know what they could have done. They would probably have left. Maybe one would finish up like the birds. But maybe, we speculated, our terrific beam of light caused such a shock to whatever was there that the energy tried to get back into the tomb. The loud roar might have been the tomb moving or beginning to crack.

It was almost 3 a.m. when we trudged back down the path to our car. Janice and I returned to the church a few days later, in daylight. There seemed nothing untoward. No more dead birds were scattered in the grounds. If there had been human agents involved, outside the paranormal phenomena – black-magic ritualists, for example – there was a possibility that we had made Skidbrook church useless to them for their purposes. We indulged in hypothesis, as one always has to do in such cases. Had some group's performances at the church been the catalyst that had awakened the forces lying dormant in the church? Had this happened deliberately or accidentally? Maybe the group conjured up more than they bargained for. Or if a magical group which met there was sufficiently advanced to know that there were forces there, then because of our visit, maybe they would not be able to use them any more. I would certainly not expect to find any further happenings at Skidbrook.

How can we explain all the strange happenings of that night? Sceptics will no doubt dismiss everything as imagination, but the point is that we did see it and it did happen. I would never discount the idea that heightened emotions might play tricks on individuals. However, we all saw the greenish smoke emerging from the graves – and, for that matter, so did Mark and his friends. They did not encounter the slime-coloured erupting cloud in the church, presumably because they did not stay around long enough to see it. What could we make of this? I cannot offer a rational explanation, any more than I can for the dead bird which was bleeding one moment and desiccated the next. Was the bird really bleeding the first time? It is well known that you can look at a thing, and because you've got yourself steamed up, you make a mistake. All that I – and Andrew – can say is that we think the bird was bleeding the first time. It was certainly dried up in the end. But was it an illusion? Illusions and hallucinations can be made to seem very, very real.

Let us assume that the bird was bleeding when we first encountered it. Had some entity drawn energy from the blood to enable it to attack us later on? This is not as outrageous as it may sound. In the history of magic, blood traditionally has energy-giving powers. Everybody knows about animal and human sacrifices and it is said that you can gain tremendous energy if you can tap into the life-force contained in blood. This is nothing new:

remember the Countess of Bathory, who thought that bathing in virgins' blood would keep her eternally young and beautiful? She killed about six hundred girls. There was, of course, much more to her madness than a mere thirst for blood. She was an infamous sadist who enjoyed torturing the girls whom she brought to her castle as servants – she was homosexual and wanted only girls. The first time she discovered that she liked blood was when a servant girl was combing her hair and happened to pull it. The countess hit the girl so hard that the blood splashed onto her arm, and she thought to herself, Oh, that makes my skin look nice and white. This gave her the idea that if she acquired more blood, she could look even better.

As soon as her husband died she set about a campaign of torture and terror. In those days, the word of people in power such as the countess, was law. Whole villages of girls disappeared and there was an outcry. Eventually, the king of Hungary sent the troops in. The countess was punished by being bricked up inside a wall, with just one brick removed for her captors to hand in food. They could not execute her because she was a member of the ruling classes, but the servants who assisted in her vile deeds were decapitated. The countess lived for about four years incarcerated like this. Curiously enough, although separated by about a hundred and fifty years, the countess was a cousin of Count Vlad the Impaler, who was the inspiration for the Dracula myth. He was the son of Prince Dracule – Dracula is a diminutive of Dracule. In fact, in Transylvania, people still believe that he was a vampire. Reports have been made of sightings of Dracula's ghost rising from the lakes that surround the island of Snagov, near Bucharest.

There may be more to vampires than flesh and blood. The annals of vampire research note that an 'astral vampire' may drain the blood of its victim even when invisible to the non-clairvoyant eye. A person will be sleeping and the astral form will be sufficiently powerful to drain actual blood from them, even though the astral form is not physical in the true sense of the word. But, as in all our research into ghosts, poltergeists and so on, just because something is not visible to most people, that does not mean it is not there. For instance, we would die very quickly from radiation poisoning if a few atom bombs went off, but you cannot see the radiation. That does not stop it from being there, and scientific technology has now developed a method of detecting its presence. So maybe we could argue that this astral form of a being can be there and can produce very definite effects – just as radiation does.

Perhaps this is how the old stories about incubi and succubi grew, not just from the idea that these invisible night-time entities had sex with their victims, but that in addition, these entities could drain the energies of people in a very physical way. As Professor J.B.S. Haldane said, the universe is not only queerer than we think, but queerer than we *can* think. I do not believe that human vampires can flap away like bats, but maybe a thing can take on a floating form which gives rise to these old stories: an amorphous thought-form. Remember, scientists will confirm that reality is not hard and firm. It only has a tendency to exist. We know there is almost certainly an 'astral body' which can leave the physical body during the Out-of-Body experience – OBE for short – so it is a short leap to the hypothesis that such an astral body could acquire energy by 'vampirizing' the living, by absorbing their energy rather in the way that a living person can act parasitically on a person and make them feel drained. There is evidence that this is more than just a psychological phenomenon: some people can deplete your vital sources of energy – not necessarily deliberately – and they feel great afterwards. You may have a sort of 'human vampire' who knows exactly what it is doing and can drain you to such a degree that you collapse – or you may have an 'astral vampire' which has no physical body, but gains strength from doing the same thing. Neither is the sort of vampire which bites your neck.

To illustrate what I mean, I have to cast my mind back a couple of years, soon after the Ghostbusters came into being. Into my consulting room one day walked a woman who was, I guess, in her thirties. She had quite bad facial scarring, so she looked older than her years, but she had the remains of a prettiness and her figure was good. 'I wanted to tell somebody this story,' she said. 'Although all this happened six or seven years ago, I thought you might be interested.' Her name was Jill and she was perfectly sound, mentally. There were no neurotic inconsistencies or posturing and she was perfectly logical in every way – something which has to be borne in mind when listening to the astonishing facts of the story which she related. She began:

> I suppose it started one cold September evening in 1980. My sister and I were sitting by the fire – I was lying on the sofa – when we saw a phantom figure materialize from nowhere. It seemed to be a short man, all in black and wearing what appeared to be a black balaclava. There was nothing in the opening of the balaclava – that is, we couldn't see a face – just blackness. Obviously, we were very startled. The shape disappeared as suddenly as it had arrived and we were left feeling frightened and uneasy. I just felt it boded ill. I was more scared than my sister. I remember I shook uncontrollably, but then, I suppose I was in quite a bad way. I had recently got divorced and had only just stopped taking tranquillizers. My two children were quite young then. I was just starting to get my life back together again.
>
> It was about two weeks later that I met a bloke called Arthur. He said he remembered me, because we had met briefly once before, in a pub, but I didn't recall that. We were married soon after, which was a big mistake. For a start, he was insanely jealous. I was quite flattered at first, but it became unbearable.

Jealousy is not a good thing. It is not flattering; it means that you are regarded as an object, an ornament, something that belongs. Apparently, Arthur was a very sexy fellow and obviously unhinged. He was violently sexually attracted to Jill and one night, before they married, Jill dreamed Arthur was ill-treating her. Three days later he hit her. That should be a warning to anybody, but in spite of this Jill went ahead and married Arthur. He apologized humbly, as these people do, and promised it would never happen again. But as we know, a leopard does not change its spots.

Arthur did not change. The physical assaults and the violence of one sort or another became part of the marriage. He was a fisherman who worked intermittently and when he returned from the sea he would beat her up, accuse her of having sex with other men while he was away and when she was sufficiently distressed and exhausted, he would force himself upon her. Jill said:

> He never made love to me. It was always more like rape, and he became more violent and perverted as time went by. He would make me take part in the most obscene acts and once, although this is revolting to tell, he even locked himself in the bathroom with the dog. I never asked what disgusting things he was doing in there – it's probably too horrible to even imagine. The most curious fact in all of this violence is that I knew when he was going to attack me. I would have dreams of him abusing or beating me – and then a few days later, he would do just what I had dreamed he would. I remember that once I dreamed that Arthur hit me with a cricket bat. I was sure this couldn't happen because we didn't have a cricket bat in the house, but a few days later Arthur came home, worked himself into a fury, rushed out of the house and came back with a cricket bat which he had 'acquired' from somewhere.

Arthur beat up Jill so badly on this occasion that the police became involved. He broke Jill's nose, knocked out some of her teeth, pulled out handfuls of hair. In spite of this, astounding as it seems, Jill would not press charges against him. 'I was so afraid of him, I just couldn't think straight,' she explained. 'He seemed to have a hold over me that I couldn't break.' And as Arthur's violence increased, the black entity in a balaclava which she had seen when she was with her sister began to re-appear regularly.

At first I thought I was imagining it, because it always appeared when Arthur was having sex with me. But it became more and more frequent and stayed longer and longer. The more violent that Arthur was when he was – well, I won't call it love-making; it was more like lust-making – the more clear the black shape would be. It was as if it *enjoyed* it! As soon as Arthur began to get sexually aroused – often by thumping me or pushing me around – then IT would appear. It was horrible. When I told Arthur about it, he said I was imagining it, but then one night, he saw it too – and he was more afraid of it than me. He became convinced that it was the ghost of his brother, Jim, who had also been a fisherman, and he said his brother had been a real bad lot.

Arthur's brother, who always used to wear black, had apparently been lost at sea and whatever had happened was never satisfactorily ascertained. His decapitated head was found, but the rest of the body was never recovered. This was interesting, for Jill never did see the face of the entity. One night Jill attempted to resist Arthur's sexual advances which gave him the excuse he needed to beat her unmercifully. When she collapsed weeping, he raped her. As he raped her she screamed out loud, but not just because of the rape. For leaning behind Arthur, to be seen with utter clarity, was the entity. The attraction of Arthur's behaviour seemed to be irresistible to it. According to Arthur, violence, sex, drink and drugs had been Jim's main occupations in life – and like attracts like. The sexual terror in the couple's relationship drew Jim like a magnet. He was growing in strength, for the energies needed to feed him, as in a poltergeist phenomenon, were the highest emotions, together with the blood, sweat and tears which prevailed in Arthur and Jill's dreadful relationship. The entity was flourishing.

'Arthur was so frightened of the ghost of his brother that he often slept downstairs to avoid it,' said Jill. 'Obviously, I was glad about that, but he always came back for sex eventually. Then the most frightening thing of all happened.' As Arthur rested between bouts of sex and violence, Jill found herself paralysed with fear as she saw the entity appear in the bedroom and come closer and closer to her until she felt it on top of her. It took hold of her and as it engulfed her, she could feel it raping her.

It seemed to completely and physically penetrate me. I just couldn't move or cry out because I felt numb with horror, but finally I managed to scream. Arthur woke up and gradually the ghost seemed to dissolve and disappear. Arthur saw it, but afterwards he denied that he had seen it rape me. Still, whatever he said, he was too terrified to sleep in the bedroom for a long time afterwards. I honestly thought I was going out of my mind. I wish I had known about you at the time because I was sure no one would believe me if I told them. Who would believe that I was raped by a ghost?

Then Jill discovered that she was pregnant. It was a terrible pregnancy. Arthur's demands for sex, his violence, his physical and verbal assaults on her did not diminish. If anything, he seemed to derive a perverse satisfaction from her weakened condition. The entity continued to appear and her dreams became even more frightening.

Two dreams stand out in my memory. In one, a baby was stuck fast in a drain and I was desperately trying to pull it out. In another I dreamed of being beaten by Arthur when a strange girl arrived and helped me to defend myself. Later, when I was examining my pregnant stomach, I suddenly saw the face of this girl superimposed on my body. It was a most peculiar thing to happen. It was later that I saw a photograph of this girl and I discovered from neighbours that she had committed suicide in that house where we were living, some years before.

Now the pregnancy became progressively worse and more painful. Having given birth to two children already, Jill knew what to expect and she was no coward when it came to pain, but this was worse than anything she had ever experienced. Her doctor prescribed aspirins and suggested she was probably neurotic. Ultimately she was taken to hospital in a state of collapse, where it was discovered that she had an ectopic pregnancy and the fallopian tube had burst. Jill was more dead than alive. The hospital staff were furious with Jill's GP and suggested he should be struck off the medical register, but Jill was too ill to care. Slowly she pulled through and began to recover and as soon as she could, she announced her intention of going home. The staff tried to persuade her to change her mind, but Jill was adamant: she felt that her children needed her. Arthur was not capable of looking after them properly even if he had been inclined to do so, which he was not. The hospital said it was too early, that she was still bleeding; that she should remain under observation for some time. But she insisted, and eventually they said she could go home on condition that she remained in bed for two weeks. She readily agreed, although she knew there was little chance of this. 'Once I got home, things were back to normal, of course. Arthur was as insatiable as ever. He demanded sex a day or two after I got home, and when I said I wasn't well enough, he just attacked and raped me.'

'But,' I interrupted at this point, 'the entity didn't appear?'

'How on earth did you know that?' She looked at me in astonishment. 'No. It never appeared again.'

My reason for guessing this correctly was that without Jill the entity – brother Jim – would not find an easy source of energy replenishment. While Jill was in hospital, Jim gradually ceased to be so powerfully present. On her return from hospital, Jill was debilitated, her blood was thin and she was way below par, so the life-force which was needed and drawn upon by the vampiristic entity Jim was no longer so vitally present.

'Entities such as Jim seem to act as psychic parasites, and in the manner of the parasite, they seek an easily available feed. In some way, they seem to charge up their energy from emotional excitation, and when Arthur beat Jill, the creature could enjoy the emotional distress she was experiencing. It would also draw energy from the blood and perform as an astral vampire, so no doubt when Arthur actually drew blood, there was an even easier source of sustenance. The vital energy in blood was needed by Jim to maintain his hold over Jill, indeed, to become so physically present that he could ultimately enjoy her sexually, which was clearly his intention. But when she returned from hospital she was too depleted to be of use to him and thus the link was broken.

Jill and Arthur had the type of relationship which would have been described as 'morbid' by the late eminent psychologist and psychic researcher, Dr Violet Firth – in which the stronger partner 'shorted off' essential psychic and nervous energy from the weaker. This meant that Jill had less strength to ward off the psychic assaults of Jim than she would otherwise have done. While Arthur was draining her mentally and physically, the entity was draining her psychically, but once Jill had been removed from the presence of the entity, Arthur was not adequate for it to sustain itself.

What was clear was that this was not a possession case. Had the entity been a true possessing type, Jill's run-down condition might have actually helped it to dominate both her mind and body. But 'Jim' did not want to 'possess' Jill; the entity did not want to 'be' Jill and take over her body. It wanted to enjoy her sexually, to remain itself, apart, and to retain its own character without direct control of Jill's body but enjoying access to her.

So was it a blind force of nature? Was it the disembodied soul of a depraved individual? If the black entity had a nature as unpleasant as Arthur's it was no doubt the latter – and I do feel that Arthur was probably right: that the entity had something to do with Jim. But what about Jill's dreams? The dream about the baby in the drain was simple for Jill to interpret: it was a premonition of the ectopic pregnancy, but her understanding of the other dream came a little later, for Jill dreamed again of the girl whose face she had seen on her stomach. In the dream the girl told her she was helping; that Jill would soon be rid of Arthur for good. This puzzled Jill, for she could not see how she was to get rid of Arthur.

Then one day, months later, my parents, who lived in New Zealand and whom I hadn't seen for three years, came back to England. I was delighted to see them, but then they told me some very upsetting news. Apparently, my brother had been shot and killed. They said he had been gun-running in Australia. I had been quite close to Rob as a child – he was always big and protective – so the news came as quite a blow to me. To make matters worse Arthur would not have my parents in the house. They were old and couldn't stand up to his violence and aggression, so they left.

A few nights later, Jill's dream girl appeared for the third and last time. She told Jill that her parents had been misinformed; that her brother was not dead and that he was on his way home to England. She woke up crying, certain that the dream was merely wish-fulfilment. Meanwhile, Arthur's violence was, if anything, worse than ever. He was beginning to ill-treat the children too. 'Months later, I was in tears in the kitchen alone one day, feeling in utter despair. I had told Arthur I was going to leave him, but he had threatened to kill me if I ever did. I really couldn't see any way out. I didn't hear the back door open, but suddenly I heard a voice say, "Jill love, what on earth is the matter?" I couldn't believe it. There was Rob, my brother!'

She fell into the arms of her brother. He was no angel, but he had never been violent towards Jill. Rob was a big man, built like a professional boxer, and it seemed that although he had indeed been jailed for gun-running, obviously he had not been killed, as Jill's parents had heard. He was now out of jail. 'What's the matter, Sis?' he asked. She told him what was the matter, but immediately regretted unloading her troubles, fearful of what Arthur might say. 'What are you going to do?' asked Rob, and at this point the door opened.

'Who wants to know?' asked Arthur.

'I'm her brother,' said Rob – and the blow that knocked Arthur to the floor removed most of his front teeth. 'Get up,' snarled Rob, but Arthur, like all bullies, lay there whimpering and refused to move. Rob swore at him, then picked him up and threw him against the wall. Arthur slid down and remained on the floor, almost unconscious. Taking him by the hair, Rob yanked Arthur to his feet. 'If you ever touch my sister again,' he said, 'you're dead.' With that, he opened the door, picked up Arthur and threw him into the road.

'Arthur never did touch me again. We separated and now we're divorced. The children and I are happier than we ever have been,' she told me.

'Three cheers for your brother,' I said.

'He's a lovely lad. He loves the kids. And,' she added with a smile, 'if any more black ghosts appear, I'll know who to call.' Although she knows who to call, apart from Christmas cards, I have not heard from Jill from that time to the present day.

I think that the entity was probably the disembodied form of Arthur's brother and in the same way that nice entities – revenants – come back, no doubt nasty ones do, too. The entity and Arthur were no doubt of the same nature, so it would benefit from Arthur's obnoxious behaviour. That's a possible explanation, but there are many phenomena in the world which defy explanation. I am still utterly baffled by something which happened to me many years ago and for which, beyond noting that it was frightening and sinister, I can find no answers. This is a true and totally horrific story that happened to me, which makes me go cold whenever I think about it. I'm certain that I was very nearly killed.

At that time I was a company director and I had to go to London to an exhibition of various shoe firms. Sheila and I had booked into the Cumberland Hotel for three days and because my car had been out of order for some time, my father, who was involved in the motor trade at the time, had allowed me to borrow a car from one of the garages while my car was repaired. It was a rotten, wintry morning when we set off very early along the old A1. About half-way on our journey, when we were close to Peterborough, all of a sudden, the engine stopped. It was only about 7.30 a.m. and still dark, but by the greatest of good luck, as I imagined at the time, I was near a lay-by, so I free-wheeled into the lay-by to get off the road.

'That's fine,' said Sheila.

I knew nothing about engines. 'What a pest,' I said, but I had seen a sign for a garage about a mile back. 'You stay in the car and keep warm and I'll try and get help,' I told Sheila, and pulling my coat up around my ears I set off into the blizzard. There were no cars around and I was totally fed up. But I had gone about a hundred yards in the snow when a police car drew up next to me. The policeman in the passenger seat wound down the window.

'Is there anything wrong, Sir?' he said. They called you 'Sir' in those days.

'My car's broken down. It's down the road.'

'Oh yes, we saw it. Where are you going?' I told them about the garage and the policeman said: 'Jump in, we'll give you a lift.'

I had no thoughts of parapsychology or ghosts or spooks at that moment. I was trying to get to London, I was fed up and that was that. But actually, whatever was to happen probably began at that point. As I sat in the back of the police car, it crossed my mind briefly that the policemen looked like twins, but the thought vanished almost as soon as it arrived. We went down the dip in the road and reached an old-fashioned garage with a run-down café on the side; a lorry-drivers' place. The policemen got out of the car and I noticed they were very tall, even for policemen. A man came out of the office at the side of the garage and he looked very much like the policemen exept that he was older. He looked at me and his eyes radiated a hatred which I have never seen before or since. Oh well, I thought, you can't please everybody. The policemen looked at him and grinned. 'This gentleman's car has broken down.'

The garage man did not grin; he just looked. 'Yes?' he said.

'It's up at the top of the hill,' I said.

He nodded at his Landrover. 'Get in,' he said.

On the way, I endeavoured to make some polite conversation. 'Awful morning,' I said, but he did not reply. He just stared straight ahead through his window. We reached the car. 'That's the car,' I said and at last he spoke.

'Yes,' he said. He opened the bonnet and his head disappeared under it. It took about thirty seconds and then he closed the bonnet. 'That's it.'

'What on earth was the matter with it?' I asked, feeling mightily relieved.

His answer was odd, to say the least. 'The battery's slipped.' As I say, I was very ignorant about cars in those days, but even I knew there was no such thing as a battery slipping. I knew you could have a connection come loose, but how can a battery slip? Still, I was pleased that it was fixed.

'How much?' I asked.

'A pound,' he said. I paid and off he went. I was glad to see the back of him. By now it was daylight. I got back in the car and we set off. Our three days in London passed and on the fourth day we set off back to Grimsby. It was a nice sunny morning, about 10.30 a.m. when suddenly as we went along, the engine stopped – and we just managed to drift in to a lay-by on the opposite side of the road. It was the same lay-by.

'I don't believe this,' I said. 'That garage is so dreadful with that miserable man there, but there's no other option.' We were up at the top of the hill, so we pushed the car down the hill and we reached the garage. The gruff man came out. 'It's us again,' I said, with an embarrassed laugh.

He did not even blink. 'Yes,' he stated.

'The car won't go.'

'Right.'

He buried his head under the bonnet again and I suddenly felt a bit odd. 'I don't feel very well,' I said to Sheila.

'Look,' she said. 'There's a café. Let's see if we can get a cup of tea.'

I sat at a table while she went to the bar. There were about a dozen fellows sitting at one end of this little café – lorry-drivers, no doubt. I lit a cigar – I smoked in those days. Suddenly I fell on the floor with a crash. My cigar rolled away. Sheila came running over. I was full of pain; I couldn't breathe; I couldn't move. I was immobile, but alert enough to realize that what happened next was extraordinary. Because the men at the end of the café got up, walked over to me as I lay on the floor with my eyes open, stood round in a circle without speaking, and just looked at me. Sheila was suddenly at my side, bending over me. 'What on earth's the matter?'

'I think I must be having a heart attack,' I gasped. 'I've some terrible pains in my chest and my legs and my arms. I think I'm dying.'

With that, I saw the men look up, over to the corner, and there was the big man, the garage owner, who had just walked in. The men looked at him, looked away, then walked away from me and went and sat down again, leaving just Sheila bending over me.

'What's going on?' asked the big man.

'It's my husband,' Sheila said. 'I think he's having a heart attack.' By now, I was in the most appalling pain. I couldn't breathe, I was choking, my hands had curled up, so that my nails were sticking into the palms of my hands; my lips had rolled back off my teeth and I had gone into a totally rigid spasm. Across my chest and up and down my legs it felt as if electricity was rolling the muscles up and down; as if I was being electrocuted to death. Sheila tried to pour some tea into my mouth and it just spilled down my chin and chest. 'Can I ring for an ambulance?' asked Sheila anxiously.

The man had cold-fish slate-grey eyes with very black pupils. 'The phone is out of order,' he said.

Sheila looked panic-stricken. 'What can I do?' she asked.

'I don't know.' He turned around and left her and went back behind the bar.

At that moment I knew I was dying. But suddenly, the

door opened and another man came in. From my position on the floor I could see that he looked different from the other men in the café. This man looked down at me with brown eyes, immediately bent down and said to Sheila: 'What's going on?'

'It's my husband; I think he's dying. He's had a heart attack,' said Sheila.

'Why don't you ring for an ambulance?' asked the man.

'The phone's out of order,' she said. The man looked up from his position over me and I saw his eyes catch the eyes of the big man who stood in the corner: the garage owner.

'No,' he said. 'No, my dear, the phone isn't out of order. I'll tell you what: *I'll* ring for an ambulance.' He went over to the corner and, with the big man watching him wordlessly, he took the phone. When he came back, he said: 'There's an ambulance coming from Peterborough Hospital. I'll stay with you until it arrives.'

He stayed, talking to Sheila and when Sheila said: 'This is so kind of you, Mr ...?'

'Harris. Yes, that's right, Harris. Where do you come from?'

'Grimsby.'

'Oh, Grimsby, yes, I know Grimsby. There was an RAF camp there during the war.'

This small-talk continued until the ambulance arrived. They picked me up, put me on a stretcher. By now I was as rigid as a plank and they gave me some oxygen. The moment I got some oxygen in me, I felt better. I did not notice where Mr Harris went. I was taken to the casualty department of Peterborough General and the doctor examined me.

'That's all right,' he said. 'Have a cup of tea and you can go.'

I was amazed at his lack of concern. 'It was a heart attack, was it?' I asked.

'There's nothing wrong with your heart,' the doctor replied. 'I've no idea what it was. Perhaps it was stress.'

'But I was just sitting in a café and I fell down,' I said.

We went back to the garage where the car was still waiting, and the big man was there. He did not enquire after my health. 'It's us again,' I said. 'How much do we owe you?'

'A pound.'

'What was wrong with the car?'

'The battery had slipped.' He looked at me coldly. We paid the money and off we went, not without relief. A long time later, we went back to try to find the place but it was gone. The garage had been pulled down and new roads have now been built going past it. At the time, I did not know what to make of it at all. I thought perhaps I had strained myself pushing the car. It was only as my interest in parapsychology grew that I began to think more about it. I had heard of engines being stopped; indeed I had read about people who claimed they could stop engines. The more I began to look at these things and learn about coincidence, the more I thought it was stretching 'coincidence' a little far that the car should break down at exactly the same spot on the same road between Grimsby and London for no reason at all. The battery never 'slipped' back in Grimsby ever again.

I honestly think some force stopped the car and I think that whoever was involved in this force knew what they were doing, although I don't pretend to know their motives. But motives they had. The big man was obviously waiting for me to die there, for whatever reason. These people did not react like humans; they were like robots. Maybe they were into some form of black magic, drawing energy. All these ideas are so over-the-top, but it was an over-the-top happening. What about 'Mr Harris'? Who was he? How did he know the phone was not out of order? What did he know about these people? If he did not like these people, why was he there in the first place? I have thought about this without reaching any sensible conclusion, except to reflect that it was one of the most horrific things ever to have happened to me in my life.

4

Do You Believe in Ghosts?

There is the smell of fish and chips, fried onions and candy floss in the air as the crowd of young people cruise along the promenade at Cleethorpes, dawdling to giggle over the saucy seaside postcards here, or to finger the cheap souvenirs on display outside the gaudy shop-fronts. They pass the fortune-teller's booth bearing photographs of celebrities, all of whom – if we are to believe the words – have been astounded and amazed by the gypsy's accuracy with her crystal ball; here is a picture of the mystic herself with hooded eyes and cryptic stare. The youngsters nudge one another to enter, but eventually pass by, past the slot-machine arcades and the ice-cream stalls. The pier reaches out into the Humber, which feeds the North Sea, and out into the water trots a horse and carriage, bearing tourists. The sea reaches the horse's knees as it splashes through the shallow waves. The carriage, constructed to look like a swan, is intended to appear to be floating on the waves, but the effect is only achieved by the most vivid imagination. The girls on the pavement wear mini-skirts and psychedelic tops; the boys have long hair and 'I love Wayne Fontana' hats. It is nineteen-sixty-something and the young people are on their way to Wonderland.

Children's squeals can be heard coming from the helter-skelter and big wheel on the beach as the group finally reach their goal. Wonderland: a giant hangar of a place built in 1921; these days it is decorated on the outside with cartoons of Disney characters. Inside, it contains a feast of fairground rides: the dodgems, waltzers, sideshows and a carousel; 55,000 square feet of indoor fun. 'Let's go on the ghost train!' cries one of the youngsters and they head for the ride with its frontage showing gruesome pictures of skeletons and monsters. It is early in the day; they are the first visitors. The youngsters pile into the little carriages and to an accompanying automated banshee howl, the carriages crash through the swing doors, one after another. Inside, the blackness is spasmodically snapped by green and red lights illuminating the death's heads and mutilated corpses which swing horribly towards each little train as it passes. The girls scream as a wraith in monk's habit turns to them, revealing a grinning skull inside the cowled hood. Frankenstein's monster rises from a slab and Dracula opens the lid of a coffin. A monstrous hand gropes out towards the train as it veers around a corner and they escape by inches. And here, in this dimly lit corner, a corpse swings with a noose around its neck, face purple and bloated and eyes bulging as the carriage trundles past bearing its cargo of screaming girls and laughing boys. They gasp and cover their eyes as the body sways silently to and fro, the noose cutting into the blueberried flesh. But wait: there is something *too* realistic about this corpse. The youngsters who giggle their way from the ghost train towards the waltzers are not to know that in a short while somebody will be called upon to turn on all the lights inside the ghost train and investigate the horror factory within. For the ghost train does not usually boast a dangling corpse among its nerve-wracking novelties. This is a real corpse. It is to emerge that a sad and lonely character had hidden inside the ghost train the previous evening … and hanged himself.

Is the story a true one? Rodney, Janice, Andy and I wondered just how apocryphal was the Corpse in Wonderland tale from almost thirty years ago as we headed along the prom to answer the call of Dudley Bowers, the present owner of Wonderland, who was having a spot of bother with a ghost. Dudley had not furnished us with the ghost train story; indeed, he had never heard of it. But it was a spooky enough tale to have entered the annals of north-east fable. There were other, more verifiable, suicides in the history of Wonderland. Tony Felcey, the son of a previous owner, had killed himself using the exhaust fumes of his car fifteen years previously. But it was not this young man whose ghost had been seen in Wonderland; the figure of an elderly man had been seen by Dudley Bowers's employees – and voices had been heard. Dudley is from a fairground family. Now thirty-eight he bought Wonderland in 1980 and ran it as an entertainment centre until several years ago when it became unprofitable. Now it is used as a car auction saleroom during the week and a market on Sunday. Dudley is a successful local businessman, owning property and snooker halls in addition to a car sales business in Cleethorpes. He telephoned me, as so many people do, because he thought I might be interested in his ghost.

'It isn't as if I feel any bad vibes here,' he told me. 'This place has been very kind to me. But people have seen figures who then vanish into thin air. My brother-in-law, Mick Miller, heard a voice call his name when he was alone here one night. I sometimes get the strange feeling of not being alone when I know I am. I know the people who report these odd happenings and I believe them,' he added. 'They're not the type of people who would just make stories up.' So here the Ghostbusting team were, on a gusty autumn evening, heading towards Wonderland as the wind howled from the sea, whirling discarded fish and chip wrappers across Pier Gardens and the bleak promenade to flatten them against the closed and boarded-up shop-fronts. Apart from the 'Pier 39' discothèque at the end of the pier, Cleethorpes out of season was like a funeral parlour. Wonderland looks different these days. Gone are the Donald Duck and Pluto pictures on the outside, but inside the vast building, there are relics of the past: some of the old funfair designs remain on the back wall. The crazy house frontage is a reminder of the Wonderland conceived and begun by the Wilkies and the Felceys seventy years ago – the days of steam trains when bathing machines were on this beach.

When the team and I walked in, the big building with its tarmac floor was totally empty. At the front were huge roll-down metal doors and another pair of doors twenty feet high. The enormity of the building was more apparent when it was empty, but in Wonderland's heyday this space was big enough to have its own indoor zoo and roller-coaster ride. We learned from the staff that there had been a variety of unusual occurrences. One worker saw the ghost of an elderly man walk from a vintage Rolls Royce to the accounts office, whereupon he disappeared. Another man, known as Yorkie Steve (because he comes from York) was with a colleague when they saw the figure of a man leaning over the bonnet of a car. 'He was down at the bottom of the building,' Yorkie Steve recalled. 'We went down to see who it was and there was no one there. There is no way out of here. We searched and searched, but the man had gone. The fellow who was with me doesn't actually believe in ghosts – but he can't explain what happened.' Albert Knot, the nightwatchman, had heard someone call his name in the early hours of the morning – and his two dogs, which were with him, also reacted as if they had heard something.

One of the girls – Cath – who works in the office, went to the freezer-room one afternoon and saw someone in the room. 'I couldn't believe it,' Cath told Dudley. 'He looked just like Reuben Felcey. He stood behind me and then he just disappeared.' Reuben Felcey was the father of Tony, the young man who committed suicide. Reuben died later.

Dudley said he had not actually seen any supernatural presence. 'I would like to see the ghost,' he said. 'I like things proved to me, but I have an open mind.'

We were left alone to get on with our work and took a few boxes from the sides to sit on. It would probably be a long night. I watched as Rodney walked around the building, holding the Ion Detector ahead of him, remembering vividly the times as a boy when I had been brought to Wonderland. Rodney walked past the spot where we had bought toffee apples, past the site of the shooting gallery and the other sideshows, past the house of mirrors. 'I've got something here,' Rodney suddenly said. 'The lights are on. It's here.'

'Great,' said Janice, walking over with Andrew, and we watched Rodney casting the little device to and fro in a large arc. When he aimed it to the left, the lights went out; when he aimed it to the right, they came back on again. We pinpointed the energies in a north-west direction. This was exactly inside the area which would have been encompassed by the old ghost train and its machinery. If the stories were true, could this have been the spot where the old chap was found hanging? I remembered my ghost train trips from boyhood: the horrid thrill as the skulls leered at you and dangling things like cobwebs brushed against your face as you went along in the dark. 'I'm not frightened,' I used to say – but I didn't dare open my eyes.

When addressing a ghost or any other paranormal presence, you have to talk to it as if something is really there. The same applies to possession and multiple-personality cases. It is no good behaving as if this is simply unconscious energy emanating from a person, even if you suspect it is: you talk as if there is a ghost. Rodney kept the lit-up Ion Detector still. 'Look,' we said, 'we don't know if you can hear us, but if you can, will you try and materialize?' We turned all the lights off. Nothing happened. We would have to try something else. 'Maybe you could rap on one of these boxes?' Silence, but after a moment or two, there was a flickering effect on the Ion Detector. This was encouraging.

'We have good evidence you can hear us,' I said. No response. We decided to try a unique ·experiment. 'We understand that it is extremely difficult for you to communicate with us,' I said. 'We know that it's not like picking up a telephone. But can you move away from your present environment? If you can, please move now.' Suddenly the flickering light went out. We gazed in wonder at the machine in Rodney's hand. He moved the machine around but could not find any other responses, so he returned it to the same spot. Suddenly the light came back on again.

'The light has come back on again,' I told the ghost. 'Did you move somewhere else? Could you do that again? Try and do it again.' After a minute, the flickering light went off.

Andrew said to the ghost: 'That's interesting, why don't you come and stand here, on my left?'

'Why there?' I asked.

He pointed. 'I don't know, but this is the part of the ghost train where the cars used to come out.' It seemed as good an idea as any because there was nothing in the other direction, and Andrew, although a practical fellow, is very intuitive. Rodney carried the machine over and all of a sudden, almost exactly where Andrew was pointing, it flickered on again. We had now had three definite responses.

'We believe you can hear us and we believe you can move away from us,' I said. 'Can you go back to the other spot?' The light flickered out and stopped. There was nothing else at all. Did the energy become exhausted? Did it disappear? Was it simply fed up with the game? I can't answer those questions, but we did get enough of a response to show that it had tried to do what we had suggested it should.

We then gave the ghost in Wonderland the sort of talking-to which has become second nature to us. The aim is to settle it down and enable it to move on into further dimensions which, many believe, the dead inhabit. 'We are your friends. We are here to help. We're not frightened of you and we hope you're not frightened of us. We believe you can hear us to some degree,' I said. 'But you are on a different plane. You *can* move on.' I might add that we cannot be sure of anything, including whether a ghost actually can move on if it wishes, but the hypothesis is that it might be happier by not remaining where it is. 'You can change your perceptions of your particular reality,' we told the ghost. 'Don't be frightened. Nothing can hurt you. It is now different for you and any fear or hurt will be in your mind. There are energies around you. If you are a God-believing person, then God is with you. If you are not a God-believer, then understand that you don't need to worry; you'll be all right anyway.'

We left at about 2 a.m. Had we done any good? To be frank, we cannot always tell. So often we are called merely to investigate rather than 'bust' a ghost. Dudley was not worried about his spectral resident and many other people feel exactly the same way. They just need their ghost confirming, using the scientific methods which we have at our disposal. This was certainly the case with Maria, an elegant lady who lives in a fine old country mansion just outside Grimsby. Maria was brought up by her uncle and aunt in this beautiful house, which was built in the early nineteenth century and is surrounded by acres of land. Maria is a striking-looking woman in her mid-thirties. She is divorced and her life revolves around horses: she rides, races and breeds horses. She is also very keen on dogs and there are many labradors running around the estate. It was my son, Andy, who introduced me to Maria and she had a strange tale to tell; well, two tales actually.

The first was when, as a teenager, she returned home from boarding school. 'I arrived late and my aunt said, "Now, Maria, what kept you?" I said, "I was just patting the dog," and my aunt said, "Which dog? What are you talking about?" I said, "*Our* dog, of course. I was patting Sandy under the old apple tree." My aunt looked astonished. "Well we didn't tell you before, dear, because you were in the middle of exams and we didn't want to distress you – but Sandy's dead," she said. "He died a month ago and he's buried under the apple tree." '

The years rolled by and she forgot about this incident, more or less. Her uncle died and Maria was left alone with her aunt. There came a time when her aunt, who was then about ninety, lay dying. She had round-the-clock nursing at the house, but one night, Maria was awakened at 4 a.m. by her aunt calling to her. The house was too big for Maria to have heard her aunt shout through the house – besides, her aunt was too feeble. So it was a telepathic call. She rapidly slipped on a dressing gown and ran through the corridors of the house to her aunt's room. The nurse was sitting in the corner of the room, reading. Her aunt was lying in bed and Maria sat down beside her and took her aunt's hand in her own. Her aunt looked at her and said: 'I knew that you would come.'

Maria thought, how curious it was that her aunt knew that she was going to come. 'Then something even more curious happened,' she said. 'As I sat holding my aunt's hand, I suddenly heard footsteps coming along the corridor. This sounds incredible, but I recognized the footsteps. They were my Uncle Bill's footsteps. He had such a distinctive tread. I sat in suspense, holding my aunt's hand and looking towards the closed bedroom door. The footsteps reached the door ... and stopped. I waited for the door to open, but it didn't. And when I looked down at my aunt, she was dead. I am utterly convinced to this day that Uncle Bill came for my aunt.'

But this was not the end of the story. Maria invited the Ghostbusters to do some investigating at the house because Uncle Bill was still occasionally making his presence felt. During his lifetime, Uncle Bill had a little habit of going into the main living room, reaching up to the large, low-hanging crystal chandelier and tinkling it with his fingers. 'Since he has been gone, I have heard that chandelier tinkle in just the same way on several occasions,' she told us, adding the instruction: 'But whatever you do, don't get rid of the ghost. I want to know more about it, if it really is a ghost. In fact, I would like to *see* more of it. I was very fond of my uncle and aunt and I would love to see them from time to time.'

The room where the chandelier tinkles is on the west side of the house and has large French windows overlooking a rose garden containing ornamental statues, behind which are grass tennis courts and beyond those, fields with horses grazing. We placed our machinery in various parts of the house, but it was in that main room, where the chandelier was, that we placed the Roboghost. Rodney and Andrew carried it in between them, for it is a bulky affair. There is a computer keyboard and a television monitor, and they are set up in conjunction with each other. Rodney developed the machine – and it is delightful. It has four sensors which can be placed in appropriate parts of a building. Each sensor brings information to the machine in a different sensory mode: sound, light, vibration and temperature. It is both visual and auditory. The television screen, with its four continuous, illuminated lines representing modes one, two, three and four, offers a consistent read-out. Any changes immediately show as blips on the screen, or the line running across the screen dips down or goes up, like an electrocardiograph read-out, a scribbling line. It can also 'speak'. Its robotic voice ... if switched on – will inform us of these same changes.

Almost immediately the Roboghost 'spoke' to us. 'Paranormal vibration detected,' declared the tinny Dalek voice. There was a clear seismic response registering on the screen. We could not feel anything, but such is the Roboghost's sensitivity that it responded to something. We wondered what could be causing the vibration. If in broad daylight there was a paranormal influence in the house causing discernible tremors, it could have been a very powerful haunting indeed – and, most unusually, these events were happening while we were there. Where could the vibration be coming from? What could account for it? We moved the sensors around the room. 'Paranormal temperature loss detected!' announced the

Roboghost. We discovered cold spots and seismic responses in several parts of the room. Could these have caused the chandelier to vibrate and tinkle? But if they did, why did the chandelier not tinkle all the time? And what had caused the vibration in the first place? It was a very solid house, but as we took our equipment to other places in the house, it became clear that there was a vibration in that room only.

It seemed to be a classical ghost, a ghost which, as in the stories, will haunt a place to which the person was attached in life – and in which it appears to wish to remain. To this day, Maria hears the tinkling chandelier occasionally and she often 'feels' that Uncle Bill is there. That is something which Maria would dearly like to be the case – so could this be why she hears the chandelier tinkle? Is it psychokinesis – or has Maria produced a thought-form? It could be, but I doubt it, because Maria is just one of many people who might wish for the return of loved ones – but those loved ones do not, routinely, come back. That, of course, could mean that only a selected few are capable of producing thought-forms. However, I feel it is a ghost mainly because it was such a surprise to Maria when the chandelier first tinkled. She was very busy and had a lot of problems on with the farm at that stage, so she was not consciously wishing that her uncle would walk in and tinkle the chandelier.

What is the ghost of Uncle Bill? I think it is like the ghost of an ancestor which will haunt his own home and return from time to time: the personality, the shade of someone, a shadow of a shadow, a remnant of someone who lived in a place to which they were closely bound, for whatever reason. In the case of Uncle Bill, I would think he was passionately attached to this place, which he bought after a long and very successful career in the trawler industry. Maybe sometimes you have to haunt a place even if you do not want to; maybe your emotions keep you tied. There is circumstantial evidence that seems very good for this, but unless one has died, one cannot pretend to know precisely what it's going to be like when you're dead! I cannot tell what happens after you die, or whether you have freewill to remain in that other dimension or not, but the weight of evidence seems to show that we can, on occasions, return to the fireside we knew when alive. Indeed, some of the old fertility religions had ceremonies that were aimed at showing the 'revenants' (the returned dead) that they were welcomed and thought of kindly. One of the main festivals known to all is All Hallows E'en, now Hallowe'en, which was the time when spirits of the dead were said to leave their cold graves and for a time join those that they love. People used to light bonfires at Hallowe'en. Now they are usually lit on Guy Fawkes' Night.

So, to pose the question I am constantly asked: Do I believe in ghosts? My answer would have to be yes, of course I do. But that said, there are many different types of ghosts. I believe in the possibility of them all, but I could never say, one hundred per cent, 'Yes, that exists' or 'No, that does not.' That would not be very scientific and I am essentially scientific. I think it's important to study ghosts because one day you might meet one. One day you will probably *be* a ghost – so it's a good idea to know something about them!

Are we all going to be ghosts? Probably, but whether we will all be seen by others is an entirely different matter. Out of the number of people who die, there are very few who are seen as ghosts. Not long ago, the Catholic journal, the *Tablet*, did a poll and revealed that about one in ten people will see a ghost and report it in England. England, in fact, is one of the most 'ghost-ridden' countries in the world. I have doubts about stories of ghosts of murdered people coming back to seek their murderers – or, indeed, of the ghosts of murderers coming back to try to create a bit more havoc. I'm sure there are instances, but I do not think you can choose that easily to come back. I think it is just about as difficult to choose to be a ghost as it is to research ghosts with any certainty of finding one in any particular place.

Spiritualists interpret the presence of ghosts as being

proof of an afterlife associated with God and Heaven, and they think that if a researcher says: 'I believe', meaning: 'I think it is possible that there are things called ghosts which are the remnants of a once-living being', then that means that the person is saying he believes in God. This equation is nonsense. If a form of energy – call it a soul, spirit or what you like – happens to survive the destruction of a carnate body, that means the energy is then ex-carnate as opposed to incarnate; but it is totally irrelevant whether there happens to be some form of energy elsewhere which one may call God. It is also irrelevant whether this God-force is good, bad or indifferent to the energy from a being which has survived death. The evidence from modern research most certainly comes down very heavily on the side of existence of consciousness after death, but this evidence has nothing to say about God, whichever of the assorted religions we care to regard. One of the few good things you can say about us parapsychologists is that we're not biased against other people's differing beliefs. Most religions believe they are right and everyone else is wrong, but parapsychologists, if they are worthy of the name, should not think like that.

I do not wear rosy blinkers when it comes to looking at ghosts. We just research what we find and what we do find is that we seem to have ghosts. We are simply trying to find answers to some questions – for instance, might a phantom be a thought-form created by one's own 'spirit'? If you are a point of consciousness without a body, as people sometimes feel they are during the experience of an out-of-the-body state, is it possible to 'build' yourself a body, one which you do not need but which you create because you consider that you could not exist without it? You – as a 'spirit' – may not consider this logically and consciously, but if you are the sort of person who could not accept that you could be there without a physical shell, then perhaps you would produce a mould of yourself spontaneously. And that is one sort of thought-form. Could that be what a ghost is? There are differences between various types of ghosts. A ghost-proper might be conveying a message, for instance. In my own family I had an Uncle Harry who was a regular soldier in the First World War. He was my father's brother but was very much older than my father. On the night that he was killed at Flanders my grandmother awoke from her sleep and ran on to the landing, screaming: 'Harry's dead!' She said she knew Harry was dead because she had seen him: his ghost had appeared to her. But then consider a somewhat similar case during the last war: a young woman turned around suddenly and saw her husband – who was in the Navy – standing in the doorway of the kitchen dripping with water. She stared at him for a moment or two and then he suddenly disappeared. She broke down, cried, rang her mother and said: 'I'm sure Jack is dead. I've seen his ghost here in the house.' Her mother suggested it might have been an hallucination, but the wife was inconsolable. 'No,' she insisted. 'This is what happens when people die – I'm absolutely certain that he's dead.'

Some days later a letter came from the Admiralty and she hardly dared open it. The letter said: 'Your husband's ship has been torpedoed. He was blasted out, but was pulled from the water by his mates, unconscious. He has been in hospital in Norway and has recovered well. He will be home by the weekend.' It turned out that the moment she had seen him in the doorway was the moment he had been blasted into unconsciousness and landed in the freezing waters. But he did not die at all. We might hypothesize that if he had died, this would be yet another ghost story, like the one about my uncle, rather than a 'crisis apparition' story. And indeed, a very similar mechanism may be at work. Perhaps at the moment of death or tremendous trauma, there is a mechanism which in some way yet to be discovered – magnetically or psychically – wishes to transmit the information to those nearest and dearest. And you may not necessarily die subsequently. What it comes down to is a choice between two conflicting theories. Does the mind only exist because the brain happens to be there? Or does the mind exist in its own right as something else? In that case, when the physical body dies, then the phenomenon that we call the mind will still be there, indestructible and quite separate, only associated with the body when it is a living body but existing in its own right when the body is gone, maybe as a thought-form, but not always.

There are cases of ghosts dating back to the days of ancient Greece. The philosopher Athenodorus wrote of being disturbed by the sound of rattling chains at a house he had recently bought. He looked up to see a ghost beckoning to him and ignored it for a while. He wrote: 'It was just a ghost. I wanted to see what it was going to do next.' But eventually he paid attention and it went before him, clanking its chains in typical ghostly manner, until it reached a part of his garden where it pointed at a spot. The next day Athenodorus organized men to dig up the garden and there they found a skeleton of a slave, still wearing the chains and manacles in which it had died. They had the skeleton reburied in consecrated ground – and that was the end of the haunting.

There are many other instances of ghosts returning with a message. In the case of the Chaffin will in the United States, the ghost of the dead father returned to say there was another will. 'You will find it in the lining of my old coat which is at the farm thirty miles away,' said the ghost. The family went to the farm and found this old coat, which had been thrown away. When they ripped out the lining, they found the father's last will and testament, which divided the farm land more fairly. The ghost apparently felt guilty that his elder son had inherited everything – and came back to put things right. I think a proper ghost will often have a purpose, but many 'ghosts' are no such thing. They are place-images – like holograms or recordings – which keep playing the same story over and over again. This was the type of ghost seen by Harry

Ghostbusters: Andrew Furman, Janice Paterson, Robin Furman
and Rodney Mitchell (left to right)

Grange Farm: the scene of mysterious deaths and bizarre accidents

The small window which was the only possible access to the secret staircase at Grange Farm

Alison Richards (right) with friend Marion Smith outside their
haunted rectory where a poltergeist caused havoc

Picturesque Skidbrook Church where the Ghostbusters
encountered terrifying supernatural effects

A disturbed tombstone at
Skidbrook Church, out of
which ghostly black fog arose
prior to the team's battle with
mysterious evil forces

Mary Frost, manageress of the Shoe Factory Shop in Grimsby, who watched in amazement as an elderly man in 'Rupert Bear' trousers walked through a solid wall

The site of the old ghost train, in what used to be 'Wonderland', where a spectral figure has been seen

Ian and Gillian Lock outside their eighteenth-century pump cottage in North Cockerington, Lincs, where they heard beast-like growling and their dogs became ill and refused to go upstairs

Darren and Nikki who were plagued by a poltergeist which ransacked their home

This picture from the Ghostbusters' album shows a ghostly cowled figure in an abandoned car at the Sellafield atomic energy site. This apparition was not visible when the photograph was taken

Childminder Bessie Smith with the Ghostbusters at her home in Heston, Middlesex, which was haunted by the ghost of a little girl

The Ghostbusters with their 'Ghostmobile'

Martindale, the policeman who, when he was a council employee installing central heating in the cellar of the Treasurer's House in York below the surface of the road, heard a trumpet sound and saw a Roman battalion going past him, complete with a horse. But the figures were all apparently 'cut off' at the knees. This extraordinary sight was later seen by several members of the council. These were not ghosts but place-images, and the figures appeared to be cut off at the knees because the original surface of the Roman road which ran through the cellar was eighteen inches below the surface of the ground. These so-called 'ghosts' will replay themselves every so often until they, as it were, wear the film out. They are no more real than an old film on the television where people are talking, moving and carrying on their activities, but they cannot respond to you in any way. There is fairly good evidence that this happens from time to time in various places. With true ghosts, legs do not get cut off at the knees, but the place-image is stuck where it was.

We encountered what at first sight we might have imagined to be a place-image with our 'shoe factory' ghost. This was at the retail shop of a shoe factory in Grimsby; oddly enough, it is across the road from the flat where the Golden Man was seen by the students, and it is beneath another flat where a friend of Andy's lived. This young man – also called Andrew – and his girlfriend had some strange paranormal experiences in that flat. But more of that later; we went to the shoe factory shop to meet Mary Frost, the manageress. She is a woman in her forties who has an air of efficiency and who chatted about her experiences in a very matter-of-fact way. Locking the shop one evening, she looked through the glass door and was surprised to see 'a white-haired elderly man wearing a pullover and Rupert Bear trousers', inside the shop, walking towards her between two rows of shoes. The old man looked at her as she gazed at him in disbelief, then he turned sharply to his left and walked straight through the wall of the shop. Mary, understandably, was shaken; 'but

I didn't feel scared or threatened because there didn't seem to be anything unpleasant about the old fellow,' she said. Nobody was afraid of the Rupert Bear ghost – or wished to be rid of it – yet when the team and I chatted to the other women who worked there, it seemed that virtually all of them had a tale to tell concerning the shop's haunting. Some had seen doors opening and closing of their own accord, others had watched as whole rows of shoes fell off the shelves for no apparent reason. There had been reports from customers that they had felt their feet being tickled when they were trying on shoes. But when they looked down, there was nothing to account for it. It seemed that the ghost liked feet or shoes, or both. That was rather unusual. Was this a ghost with a foot fetish?

Well, perhaps. Andy's friend, Andrew Lebourne – the one who told me his flat above the shop might be haunted – had found it hard to restrain his girlfriend from walking out after she felt her toes being tickled in bed one night. And it was not Andrew who was doing the tickling! Andrew told me about it one day when he was visiting Andy. 'Hey, I've got a ghost,' he said. 'What do you think of this?' He explained that he had discovered his shoes in places where he could not remember having left them, but since he had been under great pressure with exams – and after-exam celebrations – at the time, he had dismissed the incidents from his mind. He was not in the least frightened, probably because he has been friendly with my Andrew since they were small boys. He was one of the children who used to go on ghost-hunting expeditions around my house, looking for the resident ghostly nun at midnight with the lights off. (They did not have much luck, I might add, for one of the problems of all ghost-hunters – even adult ones – is that you do not find ghosts deliberately. Nothing is more guaranteed to stop all ghostly effects than looking for ghostly effects.) So Andrew Lebourne was almost as used to ghosts as my children are, and he ignored the effects at his new flat. He ignored them, that is, until his girlfriend, Jo, came to stay, and events came to a head.

Jo called him into the kitchen one day. 'I think I'm seeing things,' she said. 'I'm sure I saw a shadowy figure or a picture of some sort here in the kitchen.'

'What sort of figure?' asked Andrew.

'It was a vaguely outlined form,' said Jo. 'It seemed to move fleetingly across the room before disappearing.'

It was that night that Jo felt someone touching her feet in bed – and she ran out of the bedroom, too nervous to return. She spent the night on the sofa and it took some time to find her shoes in the morning. This, in conjunction with the incidents which occurred in the shop below, would seem to imply that the ghost did indeed have a foot fetish! We left our machinery in the shop for a couple of nights and did not pick up anything startling, other than vast temperature changes for which there was no explanation. It is well known that a sudden drop of temperature indicates presence because the ghost needs energy from somewhere and draws it from the warmth in the air. This happens particularly at seances where there are crowds of people. There is coldness and people shiver, but when the seance is over, there is an influx of energy and people suddenly feel hot.

Frankly, I do not think the movements in this shop have a lot to do with the Golden Man across the road. They may be loosely connected in the sense that this is the area where the old graveyard was situated, but there are many possible explanations for visual apparitions – thought-forms and place-images being just two of them. When you see something as ordinary as an elderly man in a pullover and tweed trousers, then that is much more likely to be a ghost. There is yet another option: sometimes people say they have experienced entering completely different worlds or a different period in time. These reports come from very reliable people – and some have even brought articles back with them as proof, such as Matthew Manning, the famous psychic. When he was young, he met the ghost of one Robert Merritt in his father's house in London. Robert Merritt, had, apparently, lived in the house in the sixteenth century and believed that he still belonged there. Manning, who was a very accomplished psychic even as a child, was perhaps more in tune with these paranormal intelligences than other people. (Manning, incidentally, is now a healer and Prince Philip is said to visit him because of this. He is also a psychic artist who can produce pictures – using both hands – in the manner of various artists, which are very difficult to distinguish from the originals; and he can do it in the dark, too.)

Merritt met Manning several times and eventually they exchanged gifts. Manning gave Merritt a twentieth-century item, and Merritt presented Manning with a loaf of bread which was as solid as a rock. When the loaf was taken to be carbon-dated at Oxford, it was shown to be 400 years old. A similar sort of story came from Bristol, where a numismatist entered some type of time-slip inside a shop which sold stamps. He bought a stamp display envelope which he later learned had not been sold since before the war. And the first he knew of this was when he returned to the shop to buy another. When the shop-owner explained the impossibility of acquiring such an envelope, he began to be suspicious of the old-fashioned girl who had served him the first time and had looked with puzzlement at the decimalized coinage he offered her.

Ghosts can, it seems, persist for considerable lengths of time and maybe the old man in Rupert Bear trousers bore some similarity to Robert Merritt. The shoe factory shop occupies the site where some cottages used to be and it is not too extreme to suggest that the old man might believe he still lives there. Robert Merritt was astonished to see Matthew Manning and actually spoke to him. He said he thought Manning was a ghost! So maybe the old man thought that the people in the shop were the ghosts and that he was the living one! Robert Merritt existed in a nine-year 'time warp' and if Matthew Manning met him outside those nine years, Merritt did not recognize him. The ghost of the old man in the shop has not acknowledged that he knows anyone there. Maybe he can see them, maybe he cannot. But if he is a former resident, then is there any logical reason why he should not go upstairs, as he would when he lived in his cottage? And if he does happen to like feet and gets a kick out of tickling people's toes, what better opportunity is there, now that it's a shoe shop?

Like attracts like. If you were the ghost of a little girl, for instance, is it not conceivable that you might enjoy being in a place where there are many other small children and plenty of toys? I ask, because this was the question I put to Mrs Bessie Smith when she called the Ghostbusters to her house in Heston. Mrs Smith is a childminder and she was becoming increasingly perturbed by ghostly appearances coupled with poltergeist-type effects in her house, especially those affecting her daughter's collection of stuffed toys. All the family had seen grey mist in the house; her daughter Sharon saw the ghostly mist come through her bedroom wall; a milk bottle top had levitated and travelled across the kitchen; doors were slammed and toys were seen to move up and down; a picture from the wall disappeared, never to be found; Bessie's son John had heard an 'evil' roar from inside a bedroom. When one of the children she cared for began to ask about the identity of a small strange girl in a particular room of the house, Bessie became even more twitchy. She called in a vicar, but he left the house white-faced and in a hurry, after venturing upstairs and having a bedroom door slammed in his face. At least he was convinced that something paranormal was going on. Bessie called the Ghostbusters.

In the normal way, for the team to travel around the country is very expensive. But it so happened that we were due down in London to make a programme with Thames TV. Also, at the time we were involved in making a film for CBS Fox, so we killed three birds with one stone and the film crew joined us at the modern semi-detached house with its postage-stamp sized front garden at the end of a quiet cul-de-sac in the shadow of Heathrow Airport. Mrs Smith opened the door to us. She was a small, smiling woman, a little on the chubby side, with curly fair hair, probably in her fifties. She was wearing rather battered jeans and a bomber jacket. Cheerfully, she ushered the large gang of us into the hall. It was instantly obvious that Bessie had an abiding passion: clocks. A cuckoo clock was on the opposite wall, and as we looked into the kitchen, we could see an ornate brass pendulum clock on the left-hand wall, at least eighteen inches in height. Downstairs I spotted about six clocks, including a beautiful, two-foot high Mickey Mouse clock in the lounge and another with a black face which showed a small gold aeroplane going round, displaying the time in most countries of the world.

To the sound of constant ticking and the occasional ear-splitting roar of jets taking off from Heathrow, we all tramped across the brown and rust-coloured carpets. Rodney and Andrew brought in the Roboghost and I carried the Probe, a single heat sensor about the size of a shoe box. It looks a little like the ghost-trap from the *Ghostbusters* film: black, with four little feet to stand on. At one end of the wooden box is a window containing an illuminated digital face which instantly records the temperature; any sudden changes in temperature can be seen – even in the dark. There is a long wire from the probe to the metal sensor, which is a sort of thermometer. Because of the wire, you can put the sensor wand in one room while you are in another room with the probe. This ensures that you are not interfering with anything – paranormal or otherwise – which may be going on in the room where you are checking the temperature.

Bessie took us into the lounge and introduced us to her 21-year-old daughter. Sharon, a small, chubby girl with long, straight fair hair, sat on the sofa, smoking and watching an afternoon soap opera on the television, wearing track-suit bottoms, a jumper and slippers. The family are very heavy smokers, which made the rooms rather smoke-filled – and the television seemed to be on permanently, from the moment that the first person in the house opened their eyes until the last person closes theirs. Sharon stared at the screen and said little as her mother listed the catalogue of strange events which had overtaken the family. It emerged that we were not the first ghostbusters to be brought in. Nine years previously, when Sharon had been only twelve or thirteen, similar effects had occurred and they had been stopped with an exorcism by DOM Robert Petitpierre, well known as an exorcist in parapsychological circles. Now, after almost a decade of calm, the ghost was up and running again. There were footsteps to be heard, bangs on the floor, objects being moved or removed completely. A pot of face cream had disappeared. 'Must be vanishing cream,' Andy muttered to me, *sotto voce*.

Bessie said: 'I'm sick and tired of this ghost, Robin. You're going to have to do something. She's inconvenient, she moves things around.' The family always called the ghost 'she'. There were, said Bessie, twenty-one instances of inexplicable events, which she had listed. 'The bedrooms go cold, we hear footsteps on the ceiling when no one is upstairs; and once we saw the apples moving – actually *moving* – in the fruit bowl! They wriggled around,' said Bessie. 'So do the toys in Sharon's room. Sometimes they are on the floor as if someone has been playing with them. My son John – who is married and doesn't live here – was here one day and saw his trainers going up and down in the air on the spot. Things have been seen by my other son, Philip, who is twenty-three and I have seen things too. The ghost opens cupboard doors in kitchen – and then there was the milk bottle top which she lifted into the air about twelve inches, and then she moved it across the kitchen and settled it down near the microwave. The ghost slams doors and walks about when strangers are here – she doesn't seem to like strangers.'

'What exactly has been seen?' I asked.

Sharon looked up. 'I walked through the ghost and so did Philip,' she said. 'It was like grey mist on the staircase and it made me feel ill and tired. It seemed to come through the wall into my bedroom and move my things around. I've heard the sound of a little child crying and watched toys go up and down in the air. Once I saw the bedclothes become flat in one spot, as if someone had just sat down.' She looked at her mother. 'And don't forget the footprints on your pillow.'

'Yes,' said Bessie. 'Philip heard a noise in my bedroom, then when we went in we found little imprints of feet on the pillow. The ghost rattled the steps while Sharon was decorating and she has taken a picture off a wall. All that was left was the empty hook. We haven't seen the picture since. One of the children whom I look after seemed to think she had seen a little girl in the house and it took a long time to persuade her to go back in the main room after that. Then at Christmas, one of the shiny balls was taken off the Christmas tree. Sharon and I both watched it hover in the air and then crash on the ground.'

This was certainly a staggering list. We plugged in all the machinery and found a cold spot in the lounge close to the window. Since the Smiths had double glazing, this was slightly odd. Led by Bessie we headed upstairs where a lot of the activity had taken place, and put the probe and the sensors into the three bedrooms and on the landing. Sharon's bedroom reminded me of the Star Trek episode called 'The Trouble with Tribbles'. Tribbles were little cuddly, teddy-bear creatures which were delightful but bred furiously. In the end they proliferated and filled the spaceship with Tribbles, whereupon Captain Kirk had to boldly go and do something about them. Here, it was as if Sharon had been invaded by cuddly toys. There must have been at least a couple of hundred of them on the furniture and all around the walls. 'We often find the toys after they have been moved – we don't always see them moving,' explained Bessie. In poltergeist behaviour, this is known as the shyness effect. This means that you can rarely see something begin to move or finish moving, but you can sometimes see it in movement or you might see it when it has arrived. Sometimes these moving objects are known as apports and they are often warm to the touch.

No sooner had we plugged in the Roboghost upstairs than a blip came on the screen, which surprised Rodney – and the film crew who also saw it. At that very moment there was a scream from downstairs. It was Sharon, who ran out and cried: 'The ashtray has just slid across the table under its own steam! I only just managed to catch it as it reached the edge of the table!' A blip on the screen, together with a moving ashtray – a coincidence? Many sceptics say that *everything* is a coincidence, but where do coincidences stop and unexplained happenings begin? A sceptic might say that when you pour a cup of tea, coincidentally tea comes out of the teapot spout. But we would say the tea comes out of the spout because there is tea in the teapot. But, of course, proving the psychic nature of so many events is very tricky.

Nothing more was detected during that day, but a little later in the evening we were downstairs and the CBS camera crew were upstairs packing up ready to leave, when a terrific crash came from the ceiling. We assumed one of the fellows had tripped over a bed – until they called down: 'Are you all right?' We went to the bottom of the stairs.

'What happened? Who tripped over the bed?' we all asked and they looked bewildered.

'What are you talking about?' said one of them. 'We heard a bang from downstairs ...' The bang had registered on our recorder and it seemed to have come from between the two floors. These were the only two oddities which occurred. Of course, we could not expect things to happen to order, just because we were there. I concluded that the problems revolved around members of the family, in particular, Sharon. She is a very nice girl, but there was clearly some considerable emotional tension there, illustrated by her heavy smoking and a weight problem. A lot of confused, strong emotions that have not managed to find a suitable outlet can result in an explosion of energy in the form of what Dr Nandor Fodor called 'a bundle of projected repressions' – which is essentially what he thought the poltergeist was. You have no physical way of expressing your frustrations, so it comes out in this mental or paranormal way – and even to this day, I still believe that the way to tackle this haunting would be to have some beneficial therapy aimed in Sharon's direction, possibly even removing her from the house for a time.

But that said, the situation could probably be put down to a combination of factors. Many questions nagged at me. The house we discovered, was near to a graveyard through which Sharon walks on her way home from work – and she told us that there was a child's grave close to the entrance of the graveyard. Had she drawn the spirit of a child to her? Mrs Smith has children in the house all the time and Sharon has this passion for keeping children's toys. Had she created a *tulpa*? Had she spontaneously produced a thought-form? And was she keeping it going? This was by no means a simple haunting. Sharon's attitude towards the ghost was ambivalent. One moment she would say she was not bothered about the ghost; then she would declare that she wanted to get rid of it. She was not nervous about the ghost, as much as puzzled – and Bessie seemed to display exactly the same mixed emotions. She 'knew' we were the experts and she wanted us to eliminate the ghost. She simply wanted to be rid of it, the way someone wants to be rid of a bad cold.

Unfortunately, this would be easier said than done. For one thing, poltergeist effects can never be eliminated. It is a fact that one can't exorcize a poltergeist. One can lessen the effects by making the people within a house understand the paranormal effects and one can alleviate their fears, but essentially one has to wait until it burns itself out, as eventually it will. Famous poltergeist cases, such as the hauntings at Enfield and Pontefract, were studied for months on end, and when the hauntings finally stopped, it was never completely certain whether they had been stopped by the investigators who had been monitoring the haunting over those months, or whether the effects would have ceased at that time in any case. Our own experience has shown that the attendance of the Ghostbusters with all their scientific equipment frequently results in a lessening of effects without our doing much more than being there. Coincidence again? I cannot really say. But one hypothesis would certainly be that Sharon may have been drawing external psychical effects to herself. These pre-existing energies may normally have no way of coming into any perceptible manifestation, but combined with Sharon's psychic energies, perhaps the ghost of a little girl was enabled to manifest and to do what maybe she would like to do, which is to go where other children are. And when Sharon got home, lo and behold, the energies did not get less, but they increased because the house was full of children and children have a great deal of spare energy. This would enable the little girl ghost to feed upon the energy and would also encourage her to remain in the house and manifest more strongly.

So my guess is that this child at Heston was a ghost who wandered back, possibly like the endearing little man on the stairs encountered by a friend in Grimsby. Elsie Smythe lived in a large, semi-detached old house in the park in the centre of town. I met Elsie when she worked as a manageress at a local supermarket where I used to go regularly. One day, she told me, she and her husband were watching a film on television about ghosts and hauntings and he said to her: 'What do you think about all this, Elsie?'

She replied: 'I don't know. Why?' and she looked at him. 'You've seen him, haven't you?' she exclaimed – and it turned out they had both seen the same little misty figure, but had never told each other about it because they were not particularly interested in parapsychology or mysticism. This little figure was often seen upstairs on the landing or on the staircase. It could have been a boy of about five, or perhaps a midget, for he was only about three feet tall. Elsie and her husband had a little boy of about three-and-a-half and naturally they never told him anything about what they came to regard as their resident ghost. In fact, they did not tell anyone because they were in that sort of world of work and society where you were not considered to be a very sound person if you talked about ghosts, which were certainly considered to be a bit airy-fairy. Their little man, they reasoned, harmed no one, they were not scared of it and just thought it a bit unusual, so what was the point of telling anyone?

During their first year in the house, they only saw their ghost half a dozen times between them, but the day came when they were redecorating and they had cleared out a bedroom. Among the furniture they had removed was a large, rather old-fashioned wardrobe. They had put it on the landing at the top of the stairs. Unfortunately, the catch on the door of this wardrobe was not too good and the door had a tendency to swing open, as the doors of old wardrobes often do. On this day, Elsie happened to look upstairs and her little boy was playing near the wardrobe. Worried that the door might open and bat him and make him fall downstairs – or indeed, that if he knocked the wardrobe, it might fall over on top of him, for it did not seem to be too stable, she said to her little boy: 'Don't play around there. You might fall down and hurt yourself, or the wardrobe could fall on you. Come down here.' She was working in the kitchen when she realized that she had not heard her little boy come downstairs, so she was sure he was disobeying her by continuing to play near the wardrobe. She turned to leave the kitchen to see what he was doing, but before she reached the door she heard a scream. In panic she ran frantically and there was her child sitting crying on the staircase. Upstairs, the door of the wardrobe had swung half-open. She seized her son in her arms. 'What on earth's happened to you?' she cried.

'The little man hit me!' he blubbed, and she said:

'What?'

'The little man slapped me! I wanted to see what was in the wardrobe and I was pulling at the door and he came out and slapped me!' cried the tot. The little man might very well have saved his life, for had the child yanked the door the whole wardrobe could have come down on top of him.

'What little man?' his mother asked.

'The little man who comes and sits on the stairs,' he said. Until that moment, she had no idea that the child had also seen the little man.

'The most amazing thing of all,' she told me, 'was that on my little boy's arm was a mark – a little hand-print. But how can I tell people this? They'd think I was mad.' However, she was delighted to tell me because she knew I was interested. The little man was a protective ghost, obviously there doing decent things. So on the whole, ghosts are not such bad old sticks – and mainly they are harmless. My own family has had more than its fair share of spooks. Almost thirty years ago, before our children were born, Sheila and I went to Scotland to visit Sheila's Aunty Janet. She lived on the island of Iona in a remote farmhouse and it was something of a family get-together for Sheila because her two cousins from Reading were also there. On our last evening, in the middle of the night Sheila got up to go to the bathroom, which was approached through the kitchen. When Sheila went into the kitchen, through another door walked a girl with heavy, long dark hair. They got into a conversation and the girl said she was Morag MacDonald. 'Ah,' said Sheila, 'then you must be my cousin. My father is your Uncle Peter.' They chatted like this for some time, then Sheila went on into the bathroom. When she came out, the girl had gone. Sheila mentioned to me that she had met Morag in the kitchen, but we thought nothing of it. We went home again and when our first daughter was born twenty-seven years ago, we called her Morag – simply because we liked the name and thought it was unusual. Morag must have been about eighteen when another aunt of Sheila's, old Aunt Ella, came to Grimsby to visit some relations. Sheila said she wanted to see her, because her aunt was old and she thought this might well be her last chance.

So we went to visit and during the conversation, Aunt Ella said:

'Now then, why did you call your eldest daughter Morag? It's a good Scottish name, but not many people know it down here.'

'Well,' said Sheila, 'we liked it. And of course, there's my cousin Morag, whom I met, and I thought she was rather nice.'

'What are you talking about?' said Aunt Ella, looking puzzled. 'What do you mean, you met your cousin Morag?'

'Well,' said Sheila, 'I met her at Aunty Janet's when we stayed there twenty-odd years ago.'

'You met her at Aunty Janet's?' asked Aunt Ella incredulously. 'Describe her.' So Sheila did and Ella said: 'You're absolutely right. That was Morag MacDonald. But she died in her twenties, forty years ago.' If Ella had not come to Grimsby, we would never have known that Sheila had met and chatted with a ghost. It makes you wonder how many times people meet ghosts and don't even realize it!

Another incident happened about twelve years ago at our home. I was shaving one bright summer's morning with the bathroom door open and I happened to glance out of the doorway on to the landing to see a little black dog trot past. At that time we had a black labrador called Winston and I absent-mindedly thought it was him. Then I thought, hang on, that dog's too small. Whose dog is it? I put the razor down and went out on to the landing. There was no dog anywhere. Just then Sheila came upstairs carrying a pile of ironing. Realizing that I had either had an hallucination or seen an apparition of a dog, I picked up my razor again and said nonchalantly: 'In regard to ghostly phenomena, have you seen anybody recently in the house?' I was careful to say 'anybody' not 'anything', because I wanted to get a genuine response and did not want to give Sheila clues as to what I had seen. We already had the ghost nun in the house, of course.

Sheila obviously thought I was talking about the nun. 'No, I haven't,' she replied, 'but I didn't bother to tell you that yesterday morning I saw something peculiar: a black dog on the landing.' Needless to say I was very surprised and we agreed that it was extraordinary. We have not seen the dog since, but when Winston was very old – just before he died, in fact – a tatty little black dog in a state of dehydration and decrepitude came into the garden with Winston, who seemed not to object to his presence.

My eldest son, Nicholas, said: 'Let's keep this little thing, because it's obviously lost and starving.' So he took it up to the bathroom and cleaned it up. I went upstairs just as he had finished bathing the dog and as he put it on the carpet and it scampered away I had a powerful feeling of *déjà vu*. My goodness, I thought to myself, it's the little dog I saw in this very place all those years ago. We still have this little dog, which we call Toby. Perhaps future events may cast their shadows backwards and there are ghosts of the past, present and future. There are, of course, those who do not believe in ghosts at all. People like Ned.

Ned Bloom worked for my cousin, Peter, who is a businessman in Newcastle. Ned worked at Peter's wholesale clothing warehouse. He was an old fellow who had worked there for so long that eventually I believe my cousin kept him on in a semi-charitable way. Peter is a fine chap. He and I were very close as boys and used to spend our holidays together, but while he does not dismiss the paranormal, he has no particular interest in it. Well, Ned had a crippled leg so he walked with a distinct and audible limp, supported by a stick. His footsteps would be heard a long way off: plunk-plonk, plunk-plonk. He was a nice old guy who had never learned to drive and always travelled by bus. He also had a superstitious habit of carrying a great deal of identification about himself, because he had a fixed idea that he was going to die on a bus. Ned was a bit of a character and he had no doubts about an afterlife. All that was nonsense, he used to say. 'When you're dead, you're dead,' said Ned. That was it. The end.

One morning my cousin arrived at work to be met by a policeman who said: 'Does a man work here by the name of Ned Bloom?' Peter said he did, of course. 'I'm very sorry to tell you, Sir, that Ned's dead,' said the policeman. Where was Ned found dead? In a bus. Well, thought Peter, that is extraordinary. That night, Peter went home and told his wife, Margaret, about Ned. Margaret knew Ned, and the couple were both sorry he had died. But as far as Peter was concerned, that was the end of the story. Until three o'clock that morning, that is, when Peter woke up, sat up in bed and wondered who the devil had come into the house, because he could hear someone coming up the stairs. As had happened to Maria with the chandelier-tinkling Uncle Bill, not only could Peter hear footsteps, but he recognized them. Plunk-plonk, plunk-plonk. He distinctly recognized the limp and the stick. Yes that's right: it was Ned. But Ned was dead. Peter sat in bed in the dark with his hair standing on end.

The footsteps reached the top of the stairs where a cupboard stood. Suddenly there was an enormous crash from the cupboard door. Peter was frozen in bed and sat there for quite some time wondering what to expect next; but nothing else happened after the door slammed. He wondered whether there was any point in waking Margaret, or even Sandra, his daughter who was about twelve years old at that time. Eventually he went back to sleep. The next morning he came down to breakfast and Sandra greeted him. 'Hello Daddy,' she said. 'What were you doing last night?'

'What do you mean?' he asked.

'You were clomping upstairs and slamming the cupboard door,' she said.

'Did you hear that?' he exclaimed. 'That wasn't me!'

At that moment Margaret came in. 'What on earth were you doing, Peter, making that racket in the middle of the night?' she asked.

He said: 'I didn't know you'd heard it. I didn't want to wake you up. I thought you were asleep.' All three of them had heard the footsteps and could confirm it.

So what did it mean? Peter hypothesized the same as I did, which was that this was Ned's way of saying: 'Look, I was wrong. Dead isn't necessarily dead. Dead's something else.' I think that's a lovely story.

5

Pazuzu and His Possessive Pals

The phone rang and a man's well-spoken voice, deep and assertive, asked: 'Is that Robin Furman?'

'Yes,' I replied.

He was hesitant. 'The – erm – ghostbuster?'

'Certainly.'

'Do you deal with possession?' I assured him that we did, indeed, try to help anyone with a paranormal problem, and there was a short silence at the other end of the phone. Then he said: 'Can I rely on your complete confidentiality?'

'Of course.'

'It's my wife,' he said. 'I believe she is possessed.'

I drew my notebook towards me. 'Tell me what has happened – from the beginning.'

His story began normally enough. His wife had been sleeping badly for some time and she had gone to the doctor, who had given her some sleeping pills. 'The pills certainly sent her to sleep, but she had the most terrible dreams. They were so bad that she said she preferred the insomnia. Then one night, she dropped off to sleep and she began to toss and turn and have some sort of a fit. I woke up, turned on the light and her eyes were rolling under her closed lids. Then suddenly they opened wide and she stared around her in the most awful, frightening way. I thought she was going mad. I rushed and called the doctor who suggested giving her some more pills. They haven't helped,' he added ominously. 'In fact, Hilary's got worse.'

'In what way?' I asked.

'Can you come to my house and see for yourself? She's having another fit now. Can you help?'

Soon Janice, Andrew and I were off in the limo, wondering what we would encounter this time. We arrived at a plush area a short distance from Grimsby. The detached house was an expensive, modern one with a prestigious car outside. A somewhat agitated man with a moustache, in his late thirties or early forties invited us into the hall. He was wearing a striped shirt in a subdued colour, open at the neck, and he was sweating slightly. He took us in with an anxious bustle. 'I can't believe what is happening,' he said in a low voice as we entered the house. His dress and accent told me that he was a professional man; later I learned that he was a partner in a large local company (discretion prevents me from revealing the nature of his profession). The same light-coloured carpet ran through the hall and up the staircase. The walls were tastefully decorated. Through an open door, I could see the kitchen. Like everywhere else, it was immaculately tidy and clean, almost obsessively clean. From the silence and orderly elegance of the house, it was clear that there were no children here.

Hilary, it seemed, had been acting oddly for some time and both she and Tom (not his real name) had tried to ignore what was happening, hoping that she would get over it, as if it was some sort of bug. However, one does not 'catch' possession syndrome, as if it is a cold, and it is certainly more difficult to get rid of. Before matters took their dramatic turn for the worse, Hilary had felt from time to time that she was being overshadowed, that she was somehow performing actions unconsciously – lighting the fire, going to the bathroom, changing her clothes, then thinking to herself suddenly: Why am I doing this? She had been anxious not to appear neurotic or mentally unbalanced and in his turn, Tom was insistent that Hilary should not become a psychiatrists' guinea-pig, to be locked up in a closed ward and studied. 'I don't want that,' declared Tom. 'I'm not having it. She's okay, except when this happens – whatever it is. I don't trust anyone because they avoid answering any of my questions.'

'Maybe what is happening is outside the professionals' experience,' I suggested, and he agreed.

'But why on earth don't they say so?' he asked. 'In the meantime, my wife's suffering.'

'Have you called in a priest?' I suggested.

'Yes, but Hilary tells him to bugger off. That's when she's not herself, of course,' he added hastily. 'She doesn't usually use bad language like that.'

He led us up the stairs to the bedroom where Hilary, in a nightdress, was lying on the double bed on her back, totally still, staring at the ceiling. There were built-in wardrobes across one wall with a dressing table in the middle. The wall-lights were rather fussy, with ornamental decorations, and very expensive-looking. Hilary was a pretty woman, pale with faded auburn hair. 'Hilary, some people have come to see you,' said her husband. She seemed not to hear him and failed to respond at all, but continued to stare at the ceiling as if no one was in the room. I approached the bed and took her wrist to check her pulse. Sometimes you can get an idea as to internal turmoil if it is erratic or racing, but it was fine.

'Hello, Hilary,' I said in a friendly voice. 'I'm Robin Furman. My friends and I have come to see if you need any help.'

'Sod off. I'm all right.'

'You don't sound all right.'

'I'm all right, I tell you,' she replied gruffly, continuing to stare at the ceiling.

'Tom tells me you aren't all right.' Suddenly she turned and fixed her eyes upon me. That may not sound very dramatic, but it was a moment which felt very hairy. Her eyes were bolting out, white around the irises, and they seemed full of threat, as if she was going to leap towards me. Her face seemed like a distorted gargoyle mask. Was I imagining that a strange force was coming from her eyes? I felt a little dizzy. I was in a roomful of people – friends – yet I felt she stared at me, as if we were weirdly alone. It was as if a demon stared from her eyes. It was ridiculous, but that was how I felt. The others looked on as I shook myself and tried again. 'Come on Hilary,' I said. 'Tell me what really is the matter.'

'I. Am. Not. Hilary,' came the slow and measured reply, each word like the crack of a whip.

'Who are you, then?' I asked. She stared at me even more fixedly, so I repeated my question.

'Sod off. I am who I am.' Then she made a mistake. 'You wouldn't know anyway.'

It is well known in exorcisms that if you can get the victims to talk and keep talking, like policemen with witnesses, sooner or later they put their foot in it.

'I wouldn't know?' I said, trying to sound casual. 'Well, try me.'

She squirmed on the bed and muttered a stream of obscenities. Tom cringed visibly. 'This isn't like Hilary,' he murmured again. 'She never uses language like this.' Hilary wriggled provocatively on the bed. Her nightdress rode up over her thighs and Tom pulled it back down again. I was getting hot under the collar. It was difficult to ignore the fact that she was a good-looking woman. She ground her teeth and Tom shook his head despairingly.

Hilary laughed harshly, but the voice was not Hilary's. 'You've lost her, Tom,' the voice grated. 'I have your wife now.' This was very strange.

'Why not let Hilary speak to us?' I said. Although I was supposed to be talking to Hilary, that was irrelevant. If this was multiple personality disorder, which is the most severe of all the neuroses, or if it was an entity or whatever the heck it was, it didn't matter. It's no use showing you don't believe whom you're talking to. That gets you nowhere.

'You can fuck off. Haven't you got it yet? I control this

body.' The harsh voice resounded around the bedroom, alien and primitive among these modern furnishings. 'And I am not leaving.' More obscenities followed.

'I don't believe you, Hilary.' I turned to Tom and said in a loud voice: 'This is a form of hysteria. I can't take this seriously. I need more proof if I'm to be convinced that this is a possessing entity.' At that point I thought the most logical explanation was multiple personality disorder in which differing personalities seem to inhabit the same body. It is possible to talk to the individual personalities and the aim of psychiatrists is to use techniques of integration to achieve a whole human being. In many cases, several personalities are intensely hostile towards the first, the original, the so-called best-integrated personality, and sometimes therapists have a terrible job discovering which personality is deemed to be the best-integrated and which personalities should be got rid of. When you are dealing with a multiple personality, you may have a quite different encephalographic read-out for each personality. And for all we know, we may all have an infinite number of personalities within us. Then again, how can you tell the difference between multiple personality disorder and a possessing entity disorder, which is also a psychic extra personality?

Modern psychiatrists such as Ralph Allison and Adam Crabtree have hypothesized that sometimes one of the personalities could be a 'spirit' – and have then treated the personality as if it were something essentially external to the person involved. They have effectively performed secular exorcisms and have settled the matter by getting rid of the 'spirit'. Mainstream psychologists, however, would never accept that idea because it does not fit into their frame of reference. In their view, such things cannot exist. Well, in other people's views these sorts of things may well exist. We must not, as Jung said, commit the fashionable error of regarding everything we cannot explain as a fraud.

Meanwhile, I was trying to keep the lines of

communication open with Hilary and what was either an extra personality created by her unconscious, or indeed, a possessing entity. I was under pressure to recognize that I was dealing with the latter. 'I am in possession of this body,' repeated the harsh voice.

I tried again. 'Well, who are you then? Are you frightened to tell me your name?' It seemed to be stung into a response.

'All right. I'll tell you,' said the entity/Hilary. 'I am Pazuzu. Pazuzu. Do you understand? Are you any the wiser?' Well, fortunately I was. I do not know the names of all the demonic entities, because there are about 100,000 or more, but there are some better known ones. I knew from my studies of ancient mythology that Pazuzu probably appeared about 3500 BC among the Sumerians who settled in southern Mesopotamia. Pazuzu was a lion-eagle monster, a demon from the desert fringes of civilization. He was a biped. His legs were gigantic eagle's claws on the paws of a lion, his face a composite eagle and lion mixed. He had huge bat-like wings on his back. There is in existence only one statue that I know of in a museum, which is about six foot high and made of black ebony. Pazuzu dwelt in dark, hot arid places and was a nasty, sexy, demonic entity, probably used as a primitive bogey man to frighten children at night: 'If you're not good, I'll send for Pazuzu.' But basically, Pazuzu was probably a destroyer who came to strike blight into lush places and into people's hearts.

I thought there was a distinct possibility that Hilary was producing these effects herself, but I did not for one second believe that she was doing it deliberately. If she were producing them herself, it was a subconscious production. We do not intend to produce nightmares that frighten us to death – no one else is dreaming except us – but still when we are asleep we produce all manner of horrors to frighten ourselves. And that aspect of our minds which produces nightmares could, to my mind, 'escape' the confines of the skull and produce something objective, outside of you. It is not supernatural: it can be done. You could produce a waking nightmare in the form of something monstrous like Pazuzu. Of course you do not mean to do it; you do not even know you are doing it. People who produce poltergeist effects do not intend to do it, and they frighten themselves as well as everyone else.

I replied that I was indeed wiser and I decided to tackle the problem head-on, acting as if I had no doubt that Pazuzu was who he claimed to be and that he had taken up residence in Hilary's body because it was somewhere to stop. I was aware that by addressing Hilary as if she was Pazuzu this might be giving the entity a spurious legitimacy, confirming that it was indeed who it claimed to be. But it was a risk that I was prepared to take because I had to keep the conversation going. Hilary continued to writhe on the bed in a very sexy way. In this confrontation with Pazuzu, the word 'sex' was never mentioned but there was a very strong atmosphere in the room of a suppressed sexuality. I never enquired of Tom about his sexual relationship with Hilary, but she was a very attractive, sensual woman. As she writhed on the bed, Tom or I from time to time had to pull down her nightdress because it kept riding up. She would throw herself about on the bed and her nightie would yank up around her thighs, and we would pull it down. Then she would contort and buck again, open her legs and close them again, fling a foot out there and an arm out here. Everyone was sweating furiously by now. Like the possessed nuns at Loudon, dramatized in the film called *The Devils*, she twisted and contorted. The nuns revealed themselves to everybody – which is, of course, what they would do if they were frustrated sexually, for one of the releases of sexual repression is exhibitionism. Hilary was there, squirming and wriggling, and had it not been for our efforts to keep her covered, she would have exposed a lot more flesh. From time to time it became embarrassing, because she would not stay under the covers: the only way to keep her there would have been to have tied her down. 'Pazuzu' was demonstrating his power over her. Or maybe if she suffered deep-seated frustration, this was being released through this behaviour, via the safety-valve of Pazuzu, saying, in effect: 'Look, it isn't really me doing this. Therefore I'm safe.'

I pursued Pazuzu. 'Why are you possessing this woman?' I asked.

'The question is pointless,' Hilary replied.

I spoke to Pazuzu again: 'I asked what *you* want and why you are who you are.'

'I am what I am and that is all.'

'But,' I protested, 'from Hilary's point of view, you are usurping her body and have no right to be there.'

'Do not talk to me about rights,' the rasping voice of Pazuzu came back. 'There is no such thing. Rights are the inventions of the priests. They enable them to have things all their own way.' This seemed to indicate a certain cleverness, either in the mind of the entity or in the unconscious, because people who are not practised in parapsychology or logic, or who do not have priestly authority to tell them what is right, would not be able to argue with it.

Janice said to Pazuzu: 'Aren't you used to living in hot, desert regions? Here it is cold, wet and inhospitable. Not a place for someone like you.'

Andrew enquired: 'Why have you come here in the first place – and how? It's a long way from ancient Mesopotamia.'

Pazuzu ignored both of them and issued a threat instead. 'Rather than leave this body I will kill it first.'

Tom went paler than ever and put his head in his hands. 'Please do be careful,' he entreated, and I turned to him.

'Don't worry,' I said reassuringly. 'The situation is under control.' Under control! Here we were, with a scene that could have come straight out of *The Exorcist*; his wife speaking with the horrific voice of a demon which now threatened to kill her. All that was missing was her head spinning round! And I was telling him the situation was

under control! Obviously, I didn't believe it. But I lied in a
good cause. 'Why don't you go into the room next door
and rest?' I suggested. 'If anything happens, we'll call
you.' I knew it would be better if he was not present
during the whole of our secular exorcism, because such
undertakings can be particularly upsetting to the loved
ones of a possessed person. Reluctantly he left and we
began on Pazuzu in earnest. They say that in the case of
possession, there are four stages which you do not
recognize until it is too late. The first is the Entry Point
when the entity first begins manifesting. Then Erroneous
Judgement, when one may be driven by an external force,
but one will rationalize, as people are prone to do when
responding to a hypnotic suggestion. They invent logical
reasons for why they are behaving in a certain way
because they cannot accept the fact that they are acting for
a reason not of their own deciding. Thirdly comes
Voluntary Relinquishing of Control, when the person
stops resisting and 'acts out' the behaviour of this force,
which is driving them in the same way as our own
unconscious can drive us. I suppose the question could be
asked whether possession is, in truth, any more than this.
Fourthly, there is Perfect Possession, when the person is
no longer acting in what we might call a rational or
reasonable manner, but is totally at the mercy of these
forces – unconscious or external, whichever you prefer.

Just as there are stages of possession, there are six stages
of classical exorcism. It begins with the very strong sense
of Presence: one will 'feel' that something is not right.
Next, if one tries to talk to the person about whom they
think the presence might be, there comes the second
stage: Pretence. The person will pretend that nothing is
the matter. Then if one pushes on, one might get to
Breakpoint, where you must break down to some degree
the reserve of the possessed person and will find out that
something is wrong. If one pushes a little further still, one
gets Voice, where you can converse with the possessing
voice. Then you will have the Clash: the battle. Finally,

you have to get rid of the possessing entity and reach Expulsion.

Turning back to the figure on the bed, I addressed Pazuzu. 'What do you expect to gain by being here?'

The word came back like the blade of a knife: 'Power.'

'That will never work,' I said. 'You can't get power here. This is no longer a primitive world like the world you come from, where people believe in such things.'

An answer shot back smartly: 'You believe in me.' This was very clever. We were in a Catch 22 situation. If we denied believing in him, the force that represented Pazuzu might resort to more extreme measures to get his own way, and he might also refuse to talk further with us. We were concerned to keep the dialogue going as long as possible. While we were conversing with the entity, we were keeping it occupied and preventing it from distressing Hilary in other directions.

'Of course we believe in you,' I said. 'We find you an interesting scientific phenomenon.' This was intended to be deprecating. There came a cry from Hilary and she whirled around on the bed as if she were a spinning top. She was on her back and flipped over on to her stomach, like an athlete. Her legs bent backwards and her head arched back too. We were fearful for her spine. It was a horrible moment and we knew we had to keep our cool for a little longer.

'Stop being so silly,' I ordered. 'You aren't impressing us with these ridiculous contortions.'

'You will find out what I can do,' chortled Hilary/Pazuzu. With that, a line of books standing upright on a nearby shelf clattered to the floor. We all jumped. We were less cool than we thought. I looked at Janice and raised my eyebrows. She gave me a tight, shaky smile.

'You can't stay in this country,' I said sharply. 'This woman will probably die – and then where will you be? It isn't easy to find people to possess in modern England.'

There was a harsh laugh. 'I found her.'

'You were lucky. You found Hilary in a vulnerable

moment. She was an easy target. It won't be so easy next time. Where will you go then?' We kept a wary eye open for any other unusual happenings. Had Pazuzu made the books fall off the shelf or was it 'coincidence'? Hilary flipped again on the bed, returning to her original position on her back, but she remained arched, her stomach in the air. She seemed to be resting on her head and her ankles. There was a long silence. The speed of Pazuzu's responses and the violence of his threats seemed to be diminishing. Were we making progress by being persistent, by not being fazed, by not giving way? It was a battle of nerves and wits. It was Clashpoint.

'You will have to leave this place, this woman and this time,' I ordered. There was silence. 'There is no room for you here.' More silence broken only by the sound of Hilary's breathing as she lay still on the bed.

Eventually there was a reply. 'You cannot send me back,' came the growl.

'You can take yourself back.'

'No. I do not know how to get there.'

'Not true,' I rejoined. 'You found your way here; you can find your way back the same way.'

'I will haunt all of you,' the voice threatened, but it suddenly lacked conviction. The voice, which had been so harsh and guttural, seemed to have weakened, to have lost power. And as the entity lost power, so we gained it. Whatever energy Pazuzu was drawing on was petering out. Tom had been petrified and now he was gone. Could the presence have been drawing from him? We, on the other hand, were sceptical, critical, determined. It wasn't having that effect on us. Instead of dominating the pair of them easily, now it was having to fight for its life.

'Be off with you. These are empty boasts,' I said with renewed vigour. 'Go now. You can't resist the force of my power. Can you feel the force of my concentrated thought-patterns burning into you? The force is becoming greater and greater. You're going to be totally destroyed if you attempt to remain.' My group knew what to do at that point. We were all concentrating on destroying the force. The power of telepathy is considerable and we were destroying the entity by combined thought. We were not concentrating to allow the entity to think we believed in it; we were not going to add to an already-existing thought-form. We were doing the opposite. We were destroying a thought-form.

Suddenly, Pazuzu said hoarsely: 'Watch out, Robin Furman. You are a more powerful magician on earth than you realize. Be careful you do not destroy yourself. One day you will bite off more than you can chew.'

I seized on this. 'Don't worry about me. I am, as you say, a very powerful magician. So for the final time, go.' I remembered some traditional magical words which I knew would reinforce the superstitious fear that the primitive entity was now displaying. 'I conjure and adjure you to depart,' I ordered. I was really getting into my stride now and was filled with confidence. It might seem a histrionic performance, but it was necessary and appropriate. I scented victory and was beginning to feel rather smug. Suddenly the woman half-rose on the bed, then collapsed, her breathing imperceptible. My smugness instantly dissipated. This was the moment when I was most frightened, for I thought she was dead. Hilary looked pale and ill. 'Oh, my God,' I murmured, thinking Pazuzu had carried out his threat. I seized her wrist and to my relief, the pulse was there. Gradually her breathing became even and she looked calm. Expulsion. Pazuzu had apparently gone as abruptly as he had originally appeared. Janice went to the door, opened it and called Tom in. 'I think she'll be all right,' I told him, putting a reassuring hand on his shoulder.

Tom looked desperately anxious as he took Hilary's hand. 'Will she stay like this? Will she be okay?' he asked.

I reassured him loudly. I wanted to make sure that if 'Pazuzu' was still anywhere around, he could hear me. 'I have forces at my command,' I declared, 'that Pazuzu could not begin to understand.'

'Neither do I,' said Tom (and truth to tell, neither did I), 'but I'm pleased that you had them. I'm amazed.' Hilary opened her eyes and smiled wanly at Tom. 'I really didn't think there was any hope,' Tom said.

For all my show of brash confidence, I was not as certain as I had appeared. I had used part of a hypnotic technique that had been successful in reintegrating cases of multiple personality disorder. 'There was no answer to the puzzle as to why Hilary should have been affected in this way. I am sure that in some cases of possession syndrome, a psychological root may be discovered, which leads to MPD, but spontaneity seems to be the rule in 'genuine' possession cases – and Pazuzu did certainly seem to have appeared spontaneously. Pazuzu never came back, so all was well and it was unnecessary to probe further into Hilary's psychological history. It appeared to be a powerful possession case – but even so, I still had doubts about whether it was, in fact, some deep psychological conflict in the woman's unconscious which was producing all the effects. Is there any way that Hilary could have known about Pazuzu; that he was a mythical Mesopotamian demonic entity? We cannot possibly know. Apparently, she later denied any knowledge not only of Pazuzu but of any sort of entity, apart from the Devil and Father Christmas. She did not know any names of mythical entities such as Choronzon or Belphagor or Leviathon or the others. Or so she said. No one knows for certain whether or not she *could* have seen the name at some time and got it into her head, and since that day was the last time I saw her, we cannot possibly find out. Had I seen her for therapy, then under hypnosis – provided she was a good subject and provided she was willing – she might have told me: 'When I was twelve, I saw a picture of Pazuzu in a book and then consciously forgot about it.' But then again, she might not have said that. We have no way of finding out for sure, but I think one will always have doubts. That does not make the phenomenon any less valid than many other things which we take for granted. For instance, man has made mistakes in understanding the way in which light works. Scientists used to think it was a wave, but now it is known that it is not necessarily a wave; it can be a particle.

It is said that during possession, the exorcist – whether priest or secular – is in danger of being possessed by the very force that he is trying to expel from the other person, as Pazuzu threatened to possess us at one stage. If the person is not very strong, this could well happen. In the case of a priest, if his faith is strong, he will not be possessed, although he might have a struggle. In the case of a secular exorcist, if he is suddenly convinced that there is a possessing entity of great power and ferocity, he could be in considerable danger of being possessed by it. And whether it happens because one suddenly becomes convinced that it has happened and then one 'possesses' oneself, or whether it is something external, is almost beside the point. Because it is the unconscious mind at work, and that is the seat of creativity.

The most widely known possession case is, of course, that of thirteen-year-old Douglass Deen in Washington in 1949, upon which the book and then the film of *The Exorcist* were based. The exorcism took about three months in reality, and was not the almost overnight battle shown in the film. It began with poltergeist effects: scratching noises in the wall, objects hurled around, pictures levitated from walls. The first minister to be called in, a Rev. M. Winston, took the boy to his own home, but when he found he could not stand the rattling of the bed, he put Douglass on the floor on a mattress. The boy fell asleep and before Mr Winston's astonished eyes, the mattress glided across the floor, like a ship in full sail, with the boy fast asleep, until it came to a halt at the far wall. Then the priest put Douglass in one of his big armchairs to sleep. Before Douglass fell asleep, the chair gently rolled across the floor, and when it reached the wall, slowly it tipped to one side until he fell out. That is a fairly typical poltergeist effect. Eventually a Jesuit priest was called in and lived with Douglass for about three months, performing thirty exorcism ceremonies while the possessing entity made the boy scream obscenities. He even screeched in Latin, which was not a language that Douglass had studied. Eventually the effects stopped. But I cannot help but wonder whether they might have stopped anyway after all that time, without the priest's intervention. One cannot answer that, of course.

I believe in possession. If you can have something which travels from the body – call it an astral self or a spirit or, in the case of Voodoo beliefs, a '*ti bon-ange*' which can be trapped in a witch-bottle – then perhaps there is something in the idea that a form of energy can amalgamate itself with somebody who is receptive to it and produce these effects to a greater or lesser strength. And maybe adolescents, in a state of emotional turmoil and flux, are at an easier stage for this sort of energy to get in. If people are not very decided one way or another, they are much easier to control than those who have their minds made up strongly.

My first encounter with an entity was not as dramatic as the Pazuzu case, but I found it far more frightening at the time. We were on holiday in Scotland, sharing a farmhouse with another family. The other family had three children and Sheila and I had our five, who were very small at the time. Our bedroom had twin beds with a table in between them. One night I awoke in the dark early hours to find my heart pounding madly. I was absolutely terrified and I thought, what on earth am I frightened of? I have since read that you can detect danger before you are awake – a selective attention of the sleeping brain, which is a mammalian response; for example, a tired mother may not wake up if a lorry crashes outside her bedroom window, but if her baby whimpers two rooms away, will be wide awake at once. I knew I was terrified, but I did not know why. I could not remember any nightmares. The curtains were closed, but as they were unlined curtains, in the dim light of the moon I could gradually see that towards Sheila's bed there was a pyramidal shape of deeper blackness. I knew instinctively that this was evil, threatening and dangerous. I did not know what to do. In those days I did not know too much about parapsychology – but I did have a good memory and I remembered some Latin exorcisms. I thought, those'll do. I'm not a believer, but I thought it was traditional, so I muttered exorcisms at the entity: 'Fundamenta egis et montibus sanctis!' which means 'Go away, in the name of the Holy Power!' Pop! It seemed to go. Sheila slept through it all, although she reminded me later that we had not liked the feeling in that room.

Entities come in all shapes and sizes – and in all sexual orientations, as I discovered when one of my students came to me after a lecture and asked if I would see him privately. I asked whether it was a psychological problem or a parapsychological one – I never charge for parapsychological problems. He said: 'It's a mixture of both.'

'Then come round and have a cup of tea and we'll talk about it,' I said. He was about thirty, working-class, and unconventional in his clothes and attitude. His wife, whom I had already met, was about the same age, small, pretty, rather chubby with shoulder-length dark hair. I liked them. I liked their way-out clothes. On the agreed day, he arrived at my house on his motor-bike. It seemed that the couple had a female lodger with whom his wife had started a lesbian affair. The other woman was, apparently, the active partner. In the beginning the man had found this relationship a source of sexual stimulation. They would have three-in-a-bed sessions and he was quite happy with this at first, because his wife was affectionate towards him, he enjoyed watching her with her lover and everything was fine. But as time went on, he found himself being excluded further and further by the homosexual passions of his wife. 'She is more interested in the other woman than she is in me,' he told me. 'Then one night this woman was away on business and I thought, great! I've got Jane to myself. But when I got into bed and tried to make love to her, she just said, "I'm sorry." She didn't want to know.

' "Why?" I asked her, and she said: "Because I have another lover."

' "But Marion's away," I said.

' "No," she replied, "another lover, apart from Marion."

'As you can guess, I was puzzled. So I asked her who it was and told her that I had never seen her with anyone else. That was when she dropped the bombshell.

' "You can't see her," she said. "She's invisible." '

He looked at me in amazement as he told me this. His wife's other lover was seemingly a female incubus. It was a lesbian sexual entity and it apparently satisfied all Jane's needs with its lovemaking. 'Do you think she's mad?' he asked me. 'Can this be possible? Is it just her imagination?'

'Have you ever seen her with this entity?' I asked.

'Well, I haven't seen the entity, of course, but she lies there in bed and gets terribly excited, moaning and thrashing about, just as if there is someone there, but they're invisible. When the other person seems to be there, Jane's weight seems to increase and the bed seems to be indented more heavily. She has orgasms,' he said with incredulity. 'I wouldn't have believed it if I hadn't seen it. But it's certainly not a turn-on for me any more because she won't allow me anywhere near her.' That would seem to indicate that she was very happy with what was going on, but what does one say? When he began his story, I thought right away that his marriage was doomed to failure. He was having another woman in bed with him who was, it emerged, taking charge of the house and he was made to feel a stranger at home. He would come in and Marion, the other woman, would say: 'I've just cleaned that floor; be careful where you're going.' The two women seemed to have a mental ascendancy over him.

I told him that as far as the entity went, I did not think it was mere sexual hysteria, because that usually happens when the person is short of sex; when they have no partner and are in a state of frustration, which his wife quite evidently was not. It was difficult to say what was happening. I recommended certain procedures to try to interfere with the process of stimulation of his wife by the invisible entity. I suggested: 'While this girlfriend is away, say to your wife, "Right, you have this entity." Then formulate in your mind a mental image of something – a gun or a knife or a flashing light.' In the end we settled on a flashing light. 'When your wife is in a thoroughly excited state, sit at the side of her, stare at where the entity is supposed to be and picture a sudden clap of thunder and flash of lightning crashing in on the spot.'

People find it hard to grasp that something which you imagine can come into this dimension and maybe, ultimately, into any dimension. Reality is a very fragile thing. It can change from fraction of a second to fraction of a second, so things you create in your own mind can develop a reality just as powerful, maybe more powerful than the apparently solid table that you see in front of you. In an occult sense we can alter reality if we know how. If the man attacked this entity – this unseen astral body – with a flash of light, I said it might do the trick. And I understand it did, to a certain degree. At a later meeting he said that his wife was very cross and accused him of interfering with what she was doing. She did not know what he had done but she knew he had done something to stop her enjoyment.

Reading between the lines of this threesome, I think they were all confused. The girlfriend wanted the wife to go away with her and leave her husband, but the wife had said she did not want to. I could see very little hope for the marriage. The husband had accepted this lesbian situation and it could have been that the wife liked women so much that she was the one who conjured up a lesbian entity for when her lover wasn't there. On the other hand, it could possibly be a possession by some sort of dead female lesbian entity.

The last that I heard, the man had left the two women in the house together. The couple had a three-year-old daughter and he took her with him. As far as I know, there is still a threesome at that house: the two women and the astral lesbian entity.

6

Randy Roy, the Passionate Poltergeist

'Who said horseshoes are lucky?' Keith Smith said wearily to his wife Margaret when he awoke one morning to find one lying next to his head on the pillow. He picked up the brass horseshoe, which he recognized as being the one which normally hung on the wall in the living room. It was warm. He looked across at the bedroom door, which was closed. Roy, it seemed, was playing another of his tricks. This was getting tiresome. Having a poltergeist as an uninvited house-guest was no joke. For a start, you could never find anything. There was the time that a key went missing and no search could turn it up. It was discovered later ... hidden in a bowl of sugar. Then there was the money which vanished from his wallet. That appeared again – after Roy had been asked politely to return it. He was not always quite so obliging and he was usually intensely irritating. That time when Roy had spent hours opening and closing the doors, turning the lights on and off and making the radio start and stop, apparently of its own accord ... very wearisome.

'At least he's been leaving me alone recently,' said Margaret. 'Maybe he's gone off me.' Keith felt still more angry with Roy when he thought how the poltergeist had even made its presence felt when he was in bed with his wife: Roy would touch her intimately and throw Margaret into a state of panic. This was doing their sex-life no good at all, Keith thought crossly as he put on his dressing-gown. Then there was the time when Keith had gone to the bathroom in the middle of the night and had returned to the bedroom to find the door closed and his pillow on the floor near the door as he went back in, placed just right for tripping him up. Roy had made it clear that Keith was not wanted in his own bedroom. If only Roy had been a real person, Keith would have thumped him. But who can thump a poltergeist? Keith sighed, picked up the horseshoe and set off downstairs to return it to its rightful place. As he opened the bedroom door, he heard a tinkling sound on the landing. He ran out, just in time to catch a glimpse of his key-ring full of keys moving slowly up the stairs of its own volition. It was the final straw. 'We must do something about this,' he said in despair to Margaret. 'I'm going to ring that ghostbuster fellow we saw on the television. And I don't care how nutty the neighbours think I am.'

And so it came to pass that my telephone rang and on the other end of the line was Keith Smith, a printer from Birmingham, asking for help with his poltergeist.

'How do you know it's a poltergeist?' I asked.

'Well, poltergeists usually throw things around, don't they?' he said. 'That's what this has been doing.'

'Give me an idea of what it's been doing,' I said.

'It throws things around the bedroom mostly. My wife Margaret had a pot of cold cream thrown at her and I've been smacked around the head with a cuddly toy. Objects just appear through the walls – the other day, a book fell through the ceiling and landed at my feet. It hides objects and then we find them in daft places. Sometimes we don't find them at all. It turns the lights on and off, it's broken a window and this morning I woke up to find an ornamental horseshoe from downstairs on my pillow. When I touched it, it was warm.' This was an interesting point. Keith was a chap who did not know the theories of parapsychology, but one of the hallmarks of something which has been 'apported' – as this had been, into the bedroom from downstairs – is that it would probably be warm. This phenomenon is reported very often.

'Anything else?'

'Well, again this morning, I looked down the stairs and saw my bunch of keys flying up through the air on their own,' he said. 'This poltergeist is driving us crazy. He's called Roy and he's a real nuisance.'

'Roy?'

'Oh yes, he's called Roy.'

'How do you know?'

'Well, one day I came home to find the words "Help Roy" smeared in face cream on the bathroom door. Another time he wrote the words "Help Roy Now" in a mixture of powder and toothpaste on the bathroom mirror.'

'Has anyone else seen this?' I asked.

'Oh yes. My wife Margaret and a number of visitors saw the writing and even now, although it's faded, it can still be made out on the mirror. I left it there to show people. And to show that we're not making these things up.'

I asked if Keith had ever seen Roy. 'No, not clearly, but Margaret has done. She has seen a figure at the top of the stairs. And we've both seen a dark figure in the garden at night, which could conceivably be Roy. I have seen shadows pass the glass door into the hall when I have been in the living room – but there's no one there.' It so happened that Keith was telephoning some weeks before the team was due to appear on 'Central Live', a Midlands-based Friday-night show which has an invited studio audience. Many of the people in the audience had experience of ghostly phenomena and we were going to be there to support them against a couple of professional sceptics. Since we were down in Birmingham, it seemed a good opportunity to go and have a look at Keith Smith's poltergeist, and Central TV decided to film us doing just that.

The house was a red-brick suburban semi in a quiet, tree-lined cul-de-sac in Erdington, which must have been a little hamlet at one stage in its history. The pre-war houses had bay windows, small front gardens and back gardens. Keith and Margaret's house looked cosy and there was a porch at the front. When they opened the door, the couple proved to be in their early thirties. They have two young children. We walked into the small hall with its warm, red-patterned carpet and could see that the living room was on the left at the front, with the dining room beyond that. Keith showed us upstairs where there were three bedrooms. The master bedroom, where so many effects had been felt, was at the back, with a gold colour-scheme. The bathroom was all in white, including the bathroom cabinet where Roy had scrawled his name in a mixture of talcum powder and toothpaste. How could a poltergeist squeeze a tube of toothpaste, you might ask. How indeed? But since poltergeists have been known to move wardrobes, people and even, in the famous Enfield haunting, rip a complete gas fire out of the wall, it seems they are capable of anything. Keith turned on the hot taps of the washbasin and bath to build up some steam in the room, and as the mirror clouded over, the words 'Help Roy Now' began to stand out clearly. The white-painted bathroom door, where Roy's first message, 'Help Roy', had been smeared in cold cream, had long since been wiped clean.

Our equipment picked up several responses in the bedroom – which were shown quite clearly on the television programme – so it seemed that the bedroom was clearly a focal point. Keith sat on the double bed with its gold bedspread and watched us at work with our Probe and Roboghost. 'There's another reason why it's a blooming nuisance,' he said. 'Not only does it keep trying to pull the duvet off the bed, but it actually tries to get into bed with Margaret and me. In fact, the other night it seemed to jump right in.' Grimly humorous this might be to many – as no doubt it was to the sceptics back at the studio – but to Keith and Margaret, this was a frightening event. 'We tried to make a joke of it at first,' said Keith. 'We called him Randy Roy and told him to go away. But he won't.' Keith looked a little embarrassed. 'He stops our love flow,' he explained. It was obviously not much fun fighting with a ghost in the bed.

Keith said he felt Roy's hand on his leg one night when Margaret had seen the poltergeist getting into their bed. Then Margaret had felt strange touches. She even felt it clamber on top of her, trying to make love to her – and she screamed. Keith was very angry because he was about to give Margaret a cuddle – and the poltergeist had beaten him to it! Then they had a tug-of-war with the duvet. The couple believed they could smell a distinctive odour when Roy was around – a fusty, old-furniture smell, was how Keith described it. One hot summer's day, the mirror in the hall steamed up for no apparent reason and a face could be seen, as if pressed against the glass – an outline of lips, nose and eye sockets. 'Another day – a Sunday,' said Keith, 'we were sitting up in bed reading the Sunday papers when, one by one, all the drawers in the room began opening and the clothes cascaded out. It looked like a bombsite. Of course, Roy never tidies up after one of these displays – *we* have to do it!' Our temperature monitor had changed. Our Probe – the wand sensor with a large digital illuminated read-out – could be seen by Central TV viewers to be changing for no reason at all. And, if it is not too boring to repeat it, a change in temperature is one of the things most frequently associated with not only poltergeist activity, but many paranormal happenings. 'Another of Roy's tricks is throwing pillows across the bedroom and hiding my hankies,' remembered Keith. 'One day I looked for my handkerchiefs all over the house, but with no luck. Margaret had insisted that they were in the usual place in the drawer, but they weren't. Later they all turned up under my pillow on the tidily made-up bed.'

The word 'poltergeist' means 'noisy or mischievous ghost' and they were so named many years ago because people thought they were ghosts. It is generally believed that they focus on one or more people in a house, frequently a teenager who is in a state of emotional turmoil and produces a bundle of energy which causes random effects. How do you stop a poltergeist? The answer is very simple: you don't. Frequently, though, and we cannot say exactly why, the effects do decrease after scientific investigators like ourselves put in an appearance. As in so many cases, we went to Birmingham mainly to study the poltergeist, rather than to 'bust' it, and our appearance seemed to defuse the intense emotional atmosphere of the situation. We explained to Keith how these things probably work – by feeding on powerful emotions – and told him there was nothing to be frightened of. Fear will certainly keep an effect like this going and probably increase it; cool it down and the effects will lessen. We went around the house, trying to communicate with Roy: 'If you're around, Roy, and you can hear us, don't be frightened,' we said. 'You have said "Help Roy" and we're trying to help you. You can move on. Try and write on the mirror to communicate with us, if you require more help.' Roy did not write on the mirror again. He seemed to fade away. We spoke to Keith later and he said it had settled down greatly, so presumably the things we told Roy worked to a degree.

As I've said before, you talk to the apparent entity as if it is there and listening. And, you know, it really does not matter if it is there or not, for part of the motive, of course, is to allow the sufferers to hear this. Poltergeists short off people. If you suggest to someone suffering from such a haunting: 'Has the poltergeist done so-and-so?' – something it has not yet done – then very often it will do it, because you have given it the idea. Poltergeists are very limited in their imagination and intelligence; they do pointless things as children might, merely to prove exactly what they can do. And similarly, if you suggest something constructive and helpful, then that will, in fact, prove to be useful because the poltergeist will pick up on your ideas. So often, the appearance of scientific investigators really does prove an inhibiting factor, but the effects which investigators do not inhibit are those which are being produced by somebody in a very considerable state of emotional distress. The word poltergeist is misleading because it is not a ghost proper. Ghosts have no real connection with emotional disturbance, as poltergeists do. Hence the famous poltergeist in the mid-1960s in lawyers' offices at Rosenheim, near Munich. Observers, who included the police and employees of the electricity board, watched as strip lights exploded, their tubes having been twisted in the sockets; they saw pictures swinging on their hooks or rotating on the wall (this was caught on a video-film which had been left running), electrical equipment failing to work and the telephone recording vast numbers of calls to the speaking clock – many more per minute than could be dialled by a human being. The focus of the poltergeist was found to be an unhappy secretary who worked in the office, and it was discovered that this had happened to her before. Only when she left the office, did the paranormal effects cease. So if poltergeist effects may be produced within the self, what about the Erdington poltergeist? It seemed to be a variation on a theme, but there did not appear to be any particular tension in the family. Then again, unless we live with a family, this is difficult to establish.

Keith Smith's haunting was small-fry compared to the Enfield one, recorded by Guy Lyon Playfair and Maurice Gross in their book *This House is Haunted*. There the girls in the family were levitated and flung through the air, once being seen to fly in front of the bedroom window by some people standing outside. There is a photograph in the book of one of the girls in flight. One daughter was found by Playfair and Gross asleep on top of a wireless. The poltergeist boiled buckets of water. At one stage the eldest daughter was trying to come downstairs and they found her stuck immobile on the stairs, with one leg pulled back behind her as if an invisible hand was pulling her leg. They had great difficulty in pulling her down. That was the greatest poltergeist haunting in England, possibly with the exception of the Pontefract poltergeist case, in which the poltergeist, named Mr Nobody by the family, seemed to have a sense of humour. When a sceptical aunt arrived to visit, declaring that she did not believe in these things and that the children were just telling lies, the lights suddenly went out and by the glow of the firelight, the fridge door was seen to open. A jug came out, floated towards the family, poised itself over the aunt's head and tipped a pint of milk over her. She went grumbling upstairs, saying it was some kind of trick, but soon there came even worse screaming from the bedroom, where one huge hairy hand had appeared over the top of the door and another had appeared near the bottom of the door. These turned out to be Aunt Maude's fur gloves with something inside swelling them up to a vast size. 'You've got the Devil in this house,' she cried and one of the hands curled into a fist and approached her threateningly. Terrified, Aunt Maude, who was a member of the Salvation Army, began to sing 'Onward Christian Soldiers' and the two hands then came together and began to beat time to the song.

These are amazing stories, and what it comes down to is that you either call everybody involved a liar – or you accept it. And why on earth should Playfair and Gross spend two years of their time making something up?

Although Playfair and Gross failed to eliminate the Enfield poltergeist, even after two years, the people in the house were grateful to them, as people are to us. No family has ever told us they were unhappy about the Grimsby Ghostbusters going in, and I know many people who have expressed their unhappiness at the responses of other people – the sceptics who look accusingly at them, as if they are inventing the story. We never do this. We told Keith Smith we believed him, which was of far more value than a sceptic going in and saying: 'You prove this to me.' We do not ask people to prove things; neither do we interrogate people. We observe for ourselves. There was no obvious reason why Keith Smith should make things up. He simply had something going on that could not be explained and he had the courage not to hide this weird thing that was happening to his family.

Roy is still occasionally making his presence felt at the Smiths' house. Recently he locked Keith in the bedroom for ten minutes. Last Christmas he gave Keith and Margaret a present.

We went up to bed and on Margaret's pillow were several little round, foil-covered chocolates. I said, 'Don't I get any, then?' – and the next night, there were some on my pillow, too! I haven't a clue where he got them from – certainly not from our house. Maybe he pinched them from next door! We ate them – they were lovely. We have heard his voice, too. Sometimes we hear him laugh; sometimes he just says 'Margaret'. I try to communicate. If ever we leave a paper and pen hanging around, he leaves messages. His writing is loopy and scroll-like: the 'R' is rolled and the 'y' is like a wine-glass. He did a self-portrait once – he only looked like a young man – and we have learned that he died of pneumonia. He says that he wants to stay – he likes the children. When he hides things these days, like the car keys just as we're about to go out, I tend to yell, 'Stop buggering about, Roy!' and the keys usually fly through the air out of nowhere and land at our feet. We found a note from him the other day, which said, 'Roy was here but now it's time to go.' He hasn't gone, though.

We had no idea why Randy Roy had appeared in the first place. Why do poltergeists affect some families but not others? For instance, you may find a poltergeist in a house where there is a very upset little girl and conclude that she is producing poltergeist effects because she is upset. However, there are lots of other equally upset little girls who do not produce poltergeist effects. It is just one of those unaccountable variables, such as why some families are musical and some are mathematical.

I had a slight misunderstanding with Mr Yeung, who called me in to one of his three restaurants in June 1990 to check out a poltergeist. For four years, there had been problems with the tills. At the end of each day, one till would always be wrong; either too short or too much. One can find all manner of explanations for a till being short, but customers would complain if you regularly short-changed them. There had been other happenings: lights going on and off, people hearing footsteps going across the ceiling in the restaurants. Mr Yeung's secretary-cashier rang me up and I went to the restaurant to meet him. He is a man of considerable intelligence, an artist, a poet and an author. 'What I don't understand,' Mr Yeung said, 'is why, when I was in my wine-cellar, some soy flew at me.' I thought he meant soy sauce and said: 'The soy from the kitchen, Mr Yeung?'

'No, the soy from the garden,' he replied. He meant soil, but in the Chinese way, he did not pronounce the 'l'! Mr Yeung had seen garden soil fly into the cellar: *through the solid wall*, clods of earth came from nowhere and hit him on the back of the neck – and this had also happened to him at his home in Cleethorpes. He was decorating the bathroom, and after cleaning up, found soil on the floor. He cleared it away, but the next day he went back into the bathroom in the morning and there was the soil again. Altogether, he cleaned it up four times that day. 'I was running up and down the ladder in my bare feet, putting polystyrene tiles on the ceiling,' he said. 'When I put the twenty-first tile on, I came down the ladder and thought, what on earth am I standing on? It was something soft.' He nodded. 'It was that soy again!'

The fact that this was happening at both his work and his home showed that the effect was connected not with a place, but a person. Mr Yeung lived with his second wife, his parents and their three children. By all accounts, Mrs Yeung was a very strong-minded character, which caused many emotional problems. The effects had begun four years ago, which was about the time he was married for the second time. Mr Yeung is a highly imaginative, highly intelligent man and I suspect he bottles up his emotions. I hypothesized that it was a psychic disturbance from unconscious mental pressure. Mr Yeung's son helped to explain this to him because his English was not that good. Now, I believe, the wife is rather more polite and Mr Yeung understands a little of what is going on. Apparently, the effects have stopped.

In families where there is a real pig of a man, poltergeist effects are rife. One recent case in Grimsby with which I am trying to deal concerns a woman who is doubly unlucky. She has a poltergeist – and a chauvinistic husband. He has not got the courage of Keith Smith. This man will neither do anything about the poltergeist himself nor allow his wife to get help, and it is destroying the family. The woman finally came to see me after missing her first appointment – she said she was afraid of her husband. She eventually turned up and said: 'I'm really terrified.' The family were hearing banging and crashing on the bedroom floor in the middle of the night. Her husband, who is a bricklayer, said it was the plumbing, but when she said: 'Why don't you fix it then?' he raged at her. However, he had confided in his son that he, too, believed something odd was afoot, but would not admit this to his wife.

'I was so frightened one night that when the two little children – who are five and six – were in bed, I heard them screaming, but I didn't dare go upstairs.' After a short silence, there has been another outbreak of banging and the sound of footsteps in the bedroom – and the effects will increase because this is a very unhappy lady, and I feel sorry for her. My opinion is that she should leave her rotten husband, but then, that's up to her.

In several of the poltergeist cases we have attended, there has been a person of somewhat limited intelligence involved. I don't mean to say they are retarded or even violent towards their families, but they have dulled sensitivity. A Right Man – always in the right. A nasty, bitter, twisted male chauvinist pig who is always right, always dogmatic and always without any original thought in any direction. These are the sort of people who will not respond to music, art, beauty or philosophy, but who might respond to a strong stimulus like a boxing-match or a cock-fight, badger-baiting or pornography. The wife or girlfriend of a Right Man has to tread on eggs to avoid upsetting him, has to make constant allowances and tries to get everything right. But you cannot get everything right for a Right Man. He will never change, of course, and sooner or later things will fall to bits, for he is always going to be a frustrated, embittered, limited personality filled with violent anti-social emotions; just the sort of person to be associated with certain types of psychic effects, usually the more limited, simplistic poltergeist type, as these emotions explode.

We see this over and over again, not in all poltergeist infestations by any means, but it is a frequent concomitant of certain types of effects, such as banging on walls and floors, clumping footsteps and so on, and these effects do not stop as rapidly as they might in more civilized establishments because of the reactions of the people who live there: the intellectual attitude of this Right Man type of person. No one is called in to help stop the effects taking place, because while they are going on, the Right Man is denying it – which makes things worse.

Poltergeists are not commonly malicious. They try to communicate, and when the Ghostbusters go in, we attempt to do the same. We attempt to establish communication with the force and we try to get a few details about why it is doing what it is doing. Is it connected with one person, or with the whole family? Maybe poltergeists are caused by a safety mechanism in the human mind, rather like a valve in a steam engine, so that when the pressure gets to a certain level, the valve allows the steam out and stops the engine blowing out. Some researchers think – validly, I believe – that some types of poltergeists are similarly produced by excess human emotional energy blowing its top, exploding in a kinetic way, producing phenomena of a non-specific sort. That is why it is usually meaningless. Typically, poltergeists might pile up cups and saucers like a little skyscraper, as if to say: 'Look what I can do.' It is the sort of thing a rather dim person would do.

As with the entire field of parapsychology, there are more questions than answers regarding poltergeists. Are they an objective force, something which exists outside of ourselves, or are the effects created merely by the excess energy of human minds, focused externally? My answer, unhesitatingly, is both. Sometimes you can produce the energy and it does nothing in particular. But sometimes there may be a type of haunt that is 'waiting' to manifest – and if somebody is producing a lot of energies, it may draw on them to produce physical effects. The 'ghost' might be able to plug into that energy provided by a person, rather as you might charge up your car battery. That is rather different to the idea that this force explodes by itself and does nothing specific.

Poltergeists can help you or plague you. There are some cases of helpful poltergeists, and mostly they do not injure. Reports show that although hard or sharp objects may fly at speed towards a person, when they make contact, the impetus is gone and the object is feather-light, causing no hurt. But some people have had this energy turned against them, such as in the cases where people have been scratched and bitten. There is a difference between these effects and the effects of possession, as seen in *The Exorcist* or, indeed, *The Entity*, because the poltergeist is not possessing you. It is using something that you are producing, not taking over your thinking and your mind, or using your body to produce the effects that it wants. Poltergeists do not do that – and for that reason you cannot zap them with a Tractron Beam. You cannot see them to zap them! The only possible solution is to alter the situation which enables the poltergeist to manifest and in that way you might just get rid of it. You *might*. But then, where does it go?

I came back from holiday at Loch Ness to find two desperate letters from Edinburgh, sent in quick succession. Bill and Norma live in their terraced house with a dog called Cindy, an elderly Chow with a gammy leg. They had such an astonishing catalogue of poltergeist effects to outline that Andy and I at once arranged to go and stay the night with them. We arrived at the high, three-storey Victorian house with its cellars. It was a quiet road and very hilly. All the houses have cellars and, indeed, explained Norma when we met her, the trouble started when she and Bill turned their cellar into a bedroom. Neither wife nor husband is very tall, although Bill is a broad chap, a private builder who does council contracts. Norma is a clerk-cashier and has been for thirty years. They have children from their previous marriages, but they do not live with them. They have been married for only four years, when Bill moved into Norma's house, bringing with him a great deal of furniture. This explained why my first impression when walking into the house was that it seemed somewhat over-furnished. There were ornaments everywhere, and down the staircase to the cellar there hung on the wall three – yes, *three*! – copies of the so-called 'Crying Boy' picture, which has a sinister reputation.

'Two years ago,' said Norma, 'we decided to turn the basement into two more rooms. We made a bedroom and a bathroom down there.' She showed us the rooms. This was a big cellar and had been luxuriously converted, as you would expect from a builder. It certainly was not a dank, dark place. 'One night we heard footsteps upstairs. Bill thought it was an intruder and he grabbed something to defend himself with and crept upstairs. I followed him, but there was nobody there. "That's strange," he said to me – and at that moment we heard someone shuffling about in the cellar, where we had just been. But when we went down, there was nothing there. We were absolutely flummoxed.'

Nothing else happened for a night or two. Then one night, Bill got up in the middle of the night to pay a visit to the bathroom and put his feet into his slippers where he had left them at his side of the bed. His slippers were full of water! 'What's going on here?' he said aloud and sleepily, Norma asked what was the matter. 'My slippers are full of water,' he said.

'Don't be ridiculous,' Norma said. They turned on the light and looked at the slippers. There was no water on the floor around them, but when Bill picked up one of the slippers, water began to drip out of it. It was filled to the brim with water. The carpet was completely dry. Several more watery things happened. Twice, the couple's slippers were found to be full of water, with no logical explanation for it – such as a leak or plumbing problem – and three times, water was found on the floor of the bedroom. The bed was found to be wet, again, for no reason, and when Norma went out in her brand new car one morning – to post the letter to me, as it happened – she popped the letter in the box and turned back to her car to find that the panel clocks had gone mad and were whirring crazily under their own steam. This was a new car! She drove straight to the garage and the mechanic said: 'I've never heard of this before. Have you got the manual?' She reached into the door pocket for the manual … and found the pocket was full of water. 'I was surprised that the electric window still worked,' said Norma. 'The manual was soaked – and it was not even raining. The mechanic was amazed.'

While that was happening to Norma, Bill had gone to work on a council job with his brother, who is a director of the firm, and as they went along in the tipper-truck, water began to drip into the cab. It was a sunny day. Suddenly there was an explosion and the back of the cab smashed to pieces. It was the hydraulic tipper mechanism. Bill and his brother narrowly missed being injured, but it caused £4,000 worth of damage – and apparently it is very rare for a tipper-truck to suffer that sort of damage. 'Once something sat on the bed when we were in the bed,' said Norma. 'We could see the bedclothes go down. Lights and other electrical equipment went on and off, drawers opened and shut on their own. Things were moved around in the kitchen – pots and pans, cups and saucers. But it was when it moved the dog clean out of the house and into the back yard that I went spare.'

Norma had been doing some spring cleaning in the bedroom downstairs in what had been the cellar, and Cindy was lying at the top of the staircase. All the doors in the house were closed. Norma called the dog down to keep her company, but she refused, which was odd, for Cindy was normally an obedient dog. However, she did have a bit of a gammy leg, so Norma thought Cindy was probably having trouble with her leg, which deterred her from coming downstairs. She went up to get the dog. 'I'll help you down, Cindy,' she said and to her absolute amazement, there was no sign of the dog. It had gone. There were no open doors anywhere and anyway, Cindy had a bad leg and could not move quickly. Norma was mystified and looked all over the house, calling the dog. Eventually, she heard Cindy whining, and discovered that she was outside in the back garden – where Norma had not even bothered to look, because the back door was closed and locked and she knew the dog could not get outside. But there it was. Norma was utterly perplexed. 'How can I tell anyone about this?' she said. 'No one will believe me. They'll think I'm crazy.'

Now, in every household, things 'disappear' and turn up again. We all recognize the experience of losing objects which turn up later – it's a normal phenomenon which can be dismissed as absent-mindedness. But mostly people do not become so uptight about it that they go to the trouble of telling others and drawing attention to these disappearances. So the people who do report such events to the Ghostbusters cannot be dismissed so easily. They clearly recognize that these disappearances are not run-of-the-mill happenings – as did Norma and Bill. The couple continued to hear footsteps. When they were downstairs, the footsteps would be upstairs; when upstairs, they would be downstairs. One evening, Bill suddenly said to Norma: 'Move!' As she moved quickly, the living-room chandelier came away from the ceiling and hung there, suspended only by its wires. 'I always feel as if someone is in the house, and I even felt I was helped and comforted once when I fell off a ladder,' said Norma. 'But now things are becoming frightening. It even got to my mother – and she's a very sensible lady. She was so upset one night that she went and swore at the poltergeist. "Leave my daughter alone!" she shouted. "She's a good hard-working woman who has had a hard life and now that her life is settled with a good job and a good husband, and everything is very nice, why have you come to plague her?" ' Norma laughed fondly.

It seemed as if the force was gradually building up and getting stronger and stronger. The water effects were the key. Norma's reports of water in slippers and other strange places made me conclude that this was certainly a good old-fashioned poltergeist, and not just something that was imagined. What Norma and Bill did not know, not being parapsychologists, is that one of the most frequently reported modern poltergeists is a water poltergeist. Poltergeists have been around for hundreds of years and in the olden days, before houses had running water, poltergeists used to throw things about, including odiferous material, smear the walls with excrement and so on. With the advent of covered latrines and better hygiene, poltergeists began using what was most easily available. In the Enfield poltergeist case, the investigators placed a half-full bucket of water on the floor, and when they returned to the room after an hour, it was flowing over – with no rational explanation. Many investigators have found water dripping through ceilings, when there are no problems with plumbing.

We sat up until midnight and Norma told me an interesting story. As a girl of eighteen, she had met a medium called Mrs Roberts at a Christmas event. Mrs Roberts was telling fortunes and, Norma being with a group of friends, all the other girls said: 'Let's go and have our fortunes told.' Norma was reluctant. 'I don't believe in that sort of thing,' she said. 'I'm not going.' They accused her of being a party-pooper, so she went along with them. (We might hazard a guess that it was not that she did not believe in psychic phenomena, but that she had a residual fear of such things – which adds an emotional dimension.) Norma was silly enough to go in and say to the medium: 'I don't believe in this, you know.' Mrs Roberts, understandably, was annoyed and said something to the effect: 'Well, you will after tonight, my girl.' She told Norma that there were two people behind her – so from then on, of course, Norma subconsciously believed she had someone with her. She was a young girl at the time and she dismissed the idea – but as is well known in psychology, it is not so easy to dismiss something from the unconscious. The unconscious is misnamed; it is not unconscious at all: it is very powerful. It would be better called the 'co-conscious' mind. You cannot dismiss fears in the unconscious without great effort, which is why people have unexplained phobias about spiders, dogs, the dark – anything. And this is where hypnosis can help.

As the years went by Norma's feeling of presence would no longer be as vague, but would turn into a conscious conviction that something was there. When things went a bit wrong, there would be no *doubt* in her mind that something was there. And that would certainly produce a very powerful effect. Nothing dramatic happened until they opened up the cellar. Why should it come to a head then? Perhaps cellars are associated with ghost stories, because they are dark and spooky. Then there were the three pictures of the 'Crying Boy' in stages, one above the other, which you have to pass on the wall as you go down the stairs into the bedroom. This picture, showing a weeping child with a distraught expression, made the headlines because people claimed that fires started in rooms where they had 'Crying Boy' pictures. It became a modern myth that if you had such a picture, you would have a fire and people began getting rid of them because they believed the picture contained some energy. Even if these pictures did not have an energy they soon would have if people became convinced of the power associated with them: their own energies would cause the events.

Then again, if Norma and Bill knew of the picture's reputation, a poltergeist may have 'copied' this myth surrounding the picture. Poltergeists are usually limited in their imagination, so perhaps instead of producing fire, it produced water, which is apparently one of the most easily available substances for a poltergeist to work with. Researchers have suggested that water poltergeists work by electromagnetic condensation. They are also notoriously unimaginative and they get ideas by 'listening'. Just as our unconscious minds listen to us talking all the time without our being aware that information is being unconsciously absorbed, in the same way, this is how the poltergeist gets ideas. To illustrate, in the case of the Pontefract poltergeist, someone remarked that poltergeists were fond of tearing up photographs. Moments later, a photograph was torn in half. So, if a poltergeist can manage to cling on to an idea, then perhaps the 'Crying Boy' picture, with its notoriety for producing parapsychological events, truly had an effect.

I explained all this to Norma and advised that she remove the pictures. She promised to do so. I also told her what I believed about the power of her unconscious after it had absorbed the medium's malicious message all those years ago. Opening the basement probably re-awakened old energies on that site, which helped gradually to increase the force. That opening up contained spaces can result in these effects is certainly something which we come across frequently. I made strong suggestions of relaxation to Norma in accordance with well-known therapeutic techniques, which are designed to calm a person who is suffering a nervous or emotional upset. These techniques can help anybody after a little practice. 'Norma,' I said quietly, 'relax your brow, feel the tension gradually fading from the scalp. Now relax first your right arm and now your left arm.' In this way, one continues until the whole body is relaxed. I suggested breathing exercises to help the feeling of calmness and tranquillity and after some time, Norma's pulse slowed and she felt calm and a sense of well-being. It seemed to be working. Suddenly, we heard a row start next door. A woman's voice came to us through the wall: 'There's a poltergeist in this room!' she shrieked. We all stared at each other in astonishment and Norma said anxiously: 'I don't want it to hurt anybody.' She was obviously genuinely concerned that what had happened to her did not happen to anyone else.

Was it true? Could the poltergeist have abandoned one house and gone next door? By this time it was about 1 a.m. and it did not seem politic to go round to the neighbours and ask what was happening there. Norma and Bill went to bed and Andrew and I set up the Probe in various parts of the house. Downstairs, we put the Probe on a table in a place where it was easy to see. One sensor was at the top of the stairs and we kept with us the ghost detector – which detects the electromagnetic life-field. We passed fine black thread across the top and bottom of the staircase leading down to the cellar. This is a basic precaution, because if anyone physically walks down – sleepwalking, for instance – they break the thread without knowing it. We scattered aluminium powder all over the basement floor, on the carpet. This powder is easy to clean up and is very light, which means it can be disturbed by the slightest movement. It is certainly efficient – you could not walk on it without leaving footprints. All these precautions would eliminate any possibility of human intruders or fake effects, done for whatever reason. We had our torches and our cameras ready. There was a little thrill of anticipation as we settled down for the night. I slept – if that's the right word – on a camp bed in the front part of the cellar room and Andrew was in the other part of the room. Absolutely nothing happened all night long.

We left the next morning. A few weeks later I received a letter from Norma, asking for a Ghostbusters sweatshirt –

we sell them through our fan club. Things had been a lot better since our visit, she said, and mentioned that she had gone to see the next-door neighbours soon after we had left. They denied that anything had happened and insisted that they had never mentioned poltergeists the previous night.

What was the solution to the haunting suffered by Nikki and Darren Mortlock, a young Grimsby couple in their early twenties who had a 21-month-old baby called Daniel? At their semi-detached council house they heard footsteps on the stairs and landing and their two dogs refused to go upstairs. Instead, they would stand at the foot of the stairs, hackles up, growling into empty space. As the noises became worse and the light switches began going on and off, Darren and Nikki took fright. They called a vicar who came and blessed the house. This quietened things down for a while, but then it started again. Plugs were pulled in and out; the central heating was turned on and off. They came down one morning to find the television set turned on. And this time it affected their small son. Baby Daniel would say: 'Stephen's talking.' They knew of no Stephen. Then the child would refuse to sleep, saying he was afraid of 'The Mister'. This was chilling for Nikki and Darren. One day, after they had been out, they returned to find the spare bedroom had been ransacked. Drawers had been ripped out, posters torn down – the room was just a terrible jumble. But they could find no evidence of a break-in. They called the police, who said: 'What's been taken?'

'Nothing,' they said.

'Who else had a key?' asked the police.

'No one,' they said.

'What can we do then?' asked the police. Obviously, the answer was 'nothing'.

They called the Ghostbusters. The little house where they had lived since 1987 had a barren garden outside and it was poorly furnished inside. Darren, who is a keen biker, kept his motorcycle in an outhouse, cluttered with bits and pieces of bikes. His leather-jacketed biking friends were frequently at the house. 'I've seen ghosts before,' he volunteered when we arrived. 'I have seen the ghost of my Aunty Pat when I lived at home – although now I only see her when I'm ill or worried. But we hear people walking around upstairs here, and banging on the floor. My mate Paul was here one night and he heard it too.'

Darren's experience with his Aunty Pat showed he was obviously fey, but Nikki was more sceptical. 'I'll believe it when I see it,' she would say. However, she was worried about the baby.

'Daniel says such odd things,' said Nikki. 'The other day he suddenly said, "Everything in the house belongs to Stephen." There's no Stephen here!'

'Who lived here before?' I asked.

'It was an old man called Ben Foster – he died of cancer. There's only one funny thing that might have a connection with him,' said Nikki, 'and that's that a person who lives across the road said she saw an old man at our window when we were out one day.'

There was a stifling atmosphere in the back bedroom which had been ransacked. Darren and Nikki had stuck up the posters again. A huge and threatening poster showed a snarling, life-size tiger leaping out and there was a great deal of motorcycle equipment in there, even piled up on the window-ledge. On another wall were pictures of a unicorn, a black panther and a sexy woman. The wallpaper featured motorbikes adorned with semi-naked girls in various provocative positions. This reminder of Darren's footloose and fancy-free days was very distasteful to Nikki, needless to say, and I agreed with her. It was inappropriate in a house where a married couple lived with a small child. If Nikki felt resentful, could these sort of emotions contribute to the energies within the room? Could the energies have built up to a vortex of power which destroyed the room? We have already spoken about the power of pictures.

'Darren and I split up for a while,' confided Nikki.

'Everything was all right when he was away, but as soon as he came back, we heard the footsteps again. We hear them most evenings.'

'And I lost my bike keys once,' added Darren. 'As I was upstairs searching, they hit me on the back of the neck!'

'We lost Daniel's dummy – and found it, all iced-up in the freezer,' said Nikki. 'Another time we heard a crash on the ceiling. The chandelier was shaking and we ran upstairs, thinking the baby had fallen out of bed. But he was fast asleep.' We monitored the activity at the house, advised Nikki to take down the posters – but could do little else.

Another couple whose small child seemed to be a focus of psychic activity called us out in 1989. Paul and Maxine had five children, aged from three to twelve, but it was their five-year-old daughter Danielle who seemed to attract the attention of the poltergeist. Four months before we went, a coat-hanger flew off a chest of drawers right across Maxine's bedroom and hit Danielle in the face. We were called in when the poltergeist activity had re-erupted after a family row. To our surprise, since poltergeists are not usually present in a contented household, the family were a delightful, happy crowd. The three boys and two girls seemed to be happy children, even though the family were not wealthy, because Paul had been out of work for some time.

The couple had the usual list of common poltergeist effects, but Maxine had also seen a figure on the landing. 'And then Danielle screamed out in a voice like an old man – it was a demonic voice,' said Maxine. 'She says she has seen someone, too. She saw a man walk from the door to the side of her bed, pull a face at her and then walk out. She said it was an unpleasant old man.' Our equipment was registering a cold spot on the landing as Maxine told us of the most fearsome event yet. 'Last week, Danielle and Donna were in bed when this man came in and lifted up the bottom of the bed,' she said. 'He just shook the girls from side to side.' This was reminiscent of events that had occurred in the Enfield poltergeist case. The older children confirmed what the younger one said. I spoke to the boys, whose bedroom door was at the opposite end of the landing to that of the girls. The boys had watched in horrified amazement as the bed shook about with the girls screaming and crying and hanging on.

We went into the house half a dozen times, put up machinery and we detected effects. One day we were in the bedroom of Danielle and Donna as their mother settled the girls into bed. Janice was sitting on the bed and I was standing near the door with Maxine. Suddenly Maxine opened her eyes widely and looked over at a chest of drawers. 'Look,' she said. There was a pile of children's books on the top of the chest of drawers and before our eyes, we saw one of the books slide out from this pile, slide about two feet to the edge of the chest, slither off the end and drop to the floor. We held our breath and waited in great expectation for something else to happen, but nothing else did. As we left the house our only conclusion was that there was tension because Paul was out of work – when he got a job, things seemed to get a little better. But who can establish the real reasons?

One of our more recent cases has been at an old vicarage at Kirton Lindsey, a village near Scunthorpe. Alison Richards asked us to investigate her poltergeist which was spooking the whole family. She is a bright woman, a graduate in history and politics, who is in her final year studying law. Her husband is a dentist who has a surgery in the grounds, but unfortunately, the marriage has broken down and the couple live apart – so the family's period of residence in the rectory has been stressful. There are four children, aged between six and ten, living with Alison in the big seven-bedroomed house and the family have been pestered for four years. By now, readers will recognize the symptoms: footsteps going up the main staircase; things going missing, including one son's entire school uniform which had been laid out on a bed in a spare room and which went missing overnight – it has never turned up. But essentially, it was the same old story of an unimaginative poltergeist doing the same old things. I told you they were boring!

The early Victorian house, however, has a history. The last vicar had left seven years previously and the house had been standing empty and boarded up for three years before the Richards bought it. One of the rooms had been painted completely black and the Richards had a terrible job decorating and covering up the black paintwork. This room, in fact, was filled with the smell of gas recently, so powerful that Alison called in the Gas Board. But there was apparently nothing at all wrong with the gas fittings. The penultimate vicar had been killed in a horrific tractor accident in front of the house.

'Charlotte, who is nine, is very frightened,' said Alison. 'She won't go anywhere in the house at all on her own. Once, when the children were playing in the hall, there was a huge crash and a photograph was hurled downtairs from the landing. The children were with a babysitter on that day. We had another babysitter who never came again after she saw a cowled figure in the house. Then one day, I went to vacuum a room and the machine wouldn't work. When I pulled off the front of the vacuum cleaner, the engine had gone – completely gone! The entire motor had vanished into thin air – and it's never come back! It is quite bizarre.' Bizarre, yes, but a typical poltergeist prank, as was the fairy-cake trick which Alison told us about.

'I made these little cakes and put them in a pantry to cool,' she said. 'I left them there overnight and when I came down to the kitchen in the morning, there they were on the floor, laid out in a neat and tidy row from the pantry to the cooker, even though the pantry door was closed. I blamed the children and accused them of playing pranks but they pointed out, quite logically, that if they had got into the pantry with the cakes, they would have eaten them! Our ghost seems keen on moving things through closed doors. We put our little dog, a King Charles spaniel, into the downstairs cloakroom one night and in the morning, we found it in the kitchen. But the door of the cloakroom was still closed – and so was the kitchen door.' These effects are not experienced by just the family. When they went on holiday, a friend – Marion – came to the rectory to feed the family pets. She took the pet food from the pantry and noticed that an ironing-board was standing in the corner of the room. When she returned from feeding the pets, the ironing-board was blocking the pantry door.

The Roboghost picked up temperature changes and vibrations which started and stopped intermittently. There was obviously a great deal of emotional disturbance in the house, which will not help to lessen poltergeist effects and will, in all probability, increase them. We suggested that Alison should thread black cotton across the staircase – to rule out any physical prankster – and that she should leave a cassette recorder running at night to record any sounds, paranormal or otherwise. A scientist called Dr Konstantin Raudive claimed much success with this: he discovered that a tape recorder with a clean, new tape can pick up voices and claimed to have recorded 72,000 such voices. There are claims that Churchill and Hitler have been heard on the tapes, together with voices in many languages. Raudive says that this can be achieved in anybody's house, not just one which is said to be haunted – and it is a fun experiment to try. Where are the voices coming from? Is it the 'ethric wavelength' – which is what researchers sometimes call the subtle psychical emanations from everybody's minds? If so, then heaven knows what we may pick up psychically if we have the ability to do so.

And what of the two previous vicars at Kirton Lindsey – one of whom died tragically? Perhaps there are many forces milling around this house – emotional stress suffered by a mother and her children, a previous haunting and inexplicable energies. Alison, it is clear, needs to make a decision about her life. At the time of writing, she was trying to sell the rectory, but selling a large and expensive house during the period of a property slump is no easy task. Particularly when the house may contain an unwanted lodger ...

7

Magic!

It was the mysterious black powder which gave Mr X a clue that someone was trying to put a spell on him. Not that this crossed his mind when the powder made its first appearance, on the doorstep of his luxury house on the outskirts of the Scottish city where he and his partners operated. He had been on his way to work, had opened the front door and there it was, sprinkled liberally on the step like ebony grains of sand, roughly in the shape of a cross. He called to his housekeeper. 'There's some coal-dust on the doorstep,' he said. 'Brush it away, will you?' Then he stepped over it and strode to the car. Odd about the coal-dust, he thought to himself fleetingly ... We don't use coal. Then it was forgotten amid the day's business and property deals. A few days later the housekeeper opened the front door to find more black dust on the step. What a mess, she thought to herself, and as before, she took the broom and swept it away, off the step into the gravel path. Mr X was puzzled when she told him that evening and he looked around the roof of the porch. Could it be damaged and crumbling? Well, it looked perfectly sound to him. Perhaps he had better call in a plasterer.

Some days later Mr X came out of a business meeting with one of his colleagues. They chatted as they walked to his car but Mr X was surprised to discover that he had apparently left the driver's door of his black Mercedes unlocked. I'm getting forgetful, he thought, as he prepared to get in the car. 'Just a minute,' said his colleague. 'What's that on the seat?' It was black powder. Hello, thought Mr X – that looks familiar. 'I wouldn't sit on it, if I were you,' said his friend. 'Why not collect some and find out what it is?' Carefully, they gathered the powder into a container and sent it away for laboratory analysis. It was to be a week before they would hear about the sinister content of the powder. Meanwhile, Mr X had something else waiting for him at home. Through the post had come a squashy envelope. When Mr X opened it, out fell a child's small doll made of soft material. Its face was painted over and ugly new features had been roughly drawn. There was a thorn pushed into the doll's body.

Mr X laughed and showed his wife. 'Somebody is trying to scare me with black magic,' he said, and dropped the doll in the dustbin. But his package through the post was not the only one. Other members of his company received dolls, too: little carved wooden dolls with their throats gouged out or with needles stuck into them. More dolls were sent to Mr X. 'Burn them,' he told his wife. 'Just ignore them.' At first Mr X and his colleagues laughed. Then some of them became ill. One man learned he had developed multiple sclerosis. Another had an outbreak of boils. Someone else discovered he had a disease of the immune system. Mr X began having migraines, but did not really feel that worried. Who's worried about a migraine?

The results from the laboratory came back. There were strange ingredients in the black powder: datura, a very dangerous topical poison, which means that if you apply it, it can kill you; tetradotoxin, a poison which comes from the puffer fish or the sea-toad. Both these creatures have tetradotoxin in their skin, liver and intestines. Tetrado-toxin is a deadly neuro-toxin, one of the most poisonous substances known to mankind; laboratory studies have shown it to be 160,000 times more potent than cocaine and 500 times more powerful than cyanide. The Ancient

Egyptians knew of this poison more than 5,000 years ago and figures of puffer fish have been found on the tomb of a pharaoh of the 5th Dynasty. But who in Scotland would have such a thing, or know about it? Mr X and his associates began to get anxious. Did voodoo really exist? Could these poisons have caused any of their illnesses? Do curses work – and how does one counter them? Who could give him some answers? Guess who.

It happened that I had been up in Scotland on a poltergeist case some months previously, and by coincidence Mr X met the man whose house was haunted. He passed on my name. Mr X telephoned and within weeks Andy and I were northern-bound in the big car. We met Mr X and two of his colleagues at an exclusive restaurant in the city. There were lots of big black cars outside, so our limo fitted in well! Mr X was a swarthy fellow with slicked-back hair, not very tall but extremely broad, wearing an expensive suit, white shirt and dark tie. He was certainly not from Scotland. There was a foreign accent which I couldn't quite trace – somewhere Mediterranean, I would say. He had a very winning smile, but his eyes showed that he was a tough nut and he was utterly controlled. His colleague was extremely stout and he appealed to me because he had the sort of face which looked as if he knew everything – and I rather like clever people. You can grind your mind against them. He was English. There was also a tall, mousy-haired young man who looked like a policeman and who never spoke at all.

There were a number of people already dining at the restaurant and Mr X was obviously known there. People nodded to him and he was treated with very great respect. He pointed out some faces to me as we went in. 'You see this gentleman here: he received a doll and he's been ill.' He indicated another. 'That gentleman there was afflicted with an inability to pass water. That was after he received a doll with a thorn stuck into it. Over in that corner there,' he nodded in the appropriate direction, 'is a colleague who was sent a doll through the post. He later came up in an outbreak of boils.' Another man, he said, had a disease like Lupus, which is an immuno-defence system breakdown. A neuro-toxin could cause something like that. We sat at a table. 'I know that all this talk of spells sounds ridiculous, and I have never believed these things, but I have found out that this black powder is associated with voodoo and it seems as if someone is trying to kill us off,' Mr X said. 'We're not scared of anybody physically – we're fairly tough guys in our society – but I don't know what to do about this. So many people have become ill. Is it just coincidence or is there anything in it? I'm all right for the moment, but for how long? And what can I do? I'm worried in case the powder gets into the house.'

He was right to worry about the tetradotoxin. Voodoo death-curses are one thing; and there is a belief that the will can become susceptible and physical disease will ensue – for instance, the immune system begins to break down owing to the will of somebody else. But tetradotoxin is a very powerful poison which is used in voodoo, ground up with the skull bones from a corpse. There are various ways to apply the neat poison in Haiti: you can blow it down a person's back, drop it into a person's drink or food; perhaps go past them in a restaurant and drop it into their soup. When you get the sort of poison you can apply topically, you only have to touch the victim with it. While it would do no harm outside Mr X's front door if he was dressed to go out and if he did not believe there was magic to it, if he went out in his bare feet – to fetch in the milk, perhaps – it could be absorbed by the skin and he could kill himself. Tetradotoxin is a neuro-toxin used in chemical weapons – and it is used for turning people into zombies. Because there are, of course, such things as zombies.

No one in Haiti, where zombies enjoy the most notoriety, is frightened of zombies ... but they are very frightened of becoming zombies. A zombie is a slave. It is not dangerous – it is not anything. Zombies are not even dead; they are the undead – they are half alive and their brains are addled. In order to make someone into a zombie, the *bokor*, who is the witch-doctor, must capture the person's *'ti bon ange'*. In voodoo beliefs, a person is made up of five aspects: the *'z'etoile'*, which is the spiritual component not residing in the body, but in the universe – a person's star of destiny; the *'corps cadavre'*, which is the flesh-and-blood body; the *'n'âme'* – the spirit of the flesh which allows each cell of the body to function; and the two aspects of the voodoo soul, the *'gros bon ange'* and the *'ti bon ange'*. These two are described in a Haitian metaphor: sometimes, when standing in the late afternoon light, the body casts a double shadow made up of a dark core and a lighter penumbra like the faint halo that sometimes surrounds the full moon. This halo is the *ti bon ange* – the 'little good angel' – and the image at the centre is the *gros bon ange* – the 'big good angel'. The *gros bon ange* is the life-force which at death returns to God and becomes part of the reservoir of energy that supports all life. The *ti bon ange* is the aura, which moulds the individual's sentiments in each act he makes; it is the source of all personality, character and willpower. It is the *ti bon ange* which is targeted in voodoo sorcery because, according to the belief, it easily leaves the body, such as during sleep or during sudden fright, and can be captured in a *canari*, a clay jar which is then placed in the inner sanctum of the *hounfour* – a voodoo temple. A powerful *bokor* may, through spells, gain control of the *ti bon ange* of a Haitian who dies in a foreign land, but he may also capture the *ti bon ange* of the living, frequently using the sort of poison which has been described, causing the person to be left without intelligence or will. A car may be filled with petrol and ready to go, but it cannot go anywhere without its driver. In the same way, if you capture the *ti bon ange* and keep it prisoner, you can then drive the car – that is, the body – and you can take over. To create a zombie, the *bokor* must gain control of an individual's *ti bon ange* immediately after the death of the *corps cadavre*, because it is believed to hover around the body for seven days after death.

To turn someone into a zombie is extremely complicated,

because if you give them too much of the powder they die completely and the operation will fail. The person has to be not completely dead. And if you give them too little, you cannot get them under control – and then, of course, they have cunningly got out of being a zombie – so you have to get it just right. The person collapses with the poison and is considered to be dead because all overt signs of life are slowed to such an extent that the victim is catatonic; there are no perceptible signs of breathing and the heartbeat might be reduced to one beat a minute. This may sound unbelievable, but it is known in the West. If a doctor takes your pulse and there is no beat for thirty seconds or so, then you are thought to be dead. The *bokor* must wait for a period of time after burial – no more than eighteen hours, I believe – and then the person has to be removed from the grave. The *bokor* will go in the dead of night in secret and will dig the person out. The timing has to be exactly correct, because the person who is to become a zombie must have become conscious to a degree and he will be completely freaked out by this stage. Imagine: he has become conscious to find himself in a grave, buried alive and about to die of suffocation. So when he is taken out, he is absolutely frantic. In addition, the poison has had an effect to make him completely wild, addling his brain and usually making him very violent. The *bokor* normally has three or four other fellows with him and they beat up the person who is a zombie very badly until he can hardly move at all. He is then dragged off to the other end of the country where he is kept under control by constant doses of a drug and used as a slave to work in the fields. As long as a zombie eats no salt and as long as he is given this drug, he remains in an addled state of mind. The drug works in such a way that the zombies can understand simple instructions, but they have no will of their own so they cannot revolt against the zombie-master. Salt, presumably, counteracts the drug, for it is notorious in the annals of zombie-ism that salt must not be given or the zombie will become uncontrollable. There was a story recorded in a book by William B. Seabrook in 1929, *The Magic Island*, in which a voodoo priest used a number of zombies as cane-cutters at a huge plantation owned by the Haitian-American Sugar Company. The zombies escaped when the man's wife made the mistake of feeding them some salted peanuts. The zombies instantly realized their terrible situation and ran away.

In Haiti, the political influence of voodoo came from the top. Papa Doc Duvalier and his menacing Ton-ton Macoute secret police force, who always wore dark glasses, ruled the country by fear, torture and voodoo threats, which was how Papa Doc kept power for so long. Papa Doc was reputed to be a *bokor* who would practise black-magic rites, and when his regime was broken up, many bottles were smashed which were said to contain the souls of people who had been held in psychical bondage to him.

Two zombies have been 'saved'. One, called Clairvius Narcisse, told his story in an American newspaper in 1982. He recalled being taken sick in 1962 and taken to hospital where he was pronounced dead. 'I couldn't get enough air in my lungs,' he said. 'My heart was running out of strength. My stomach was burning. Then I felt myself freeze up. I heard the doctor tell my sister: "I'm sorry, he's dead." I wanted to cry out, to tell her that I was alive, but I was unable to move.' At his funeral he could hear his friends and relatives weeping and heard the earth falling on his coffin. The next thing he remembered was standing by the graveside in a trance-like state. Two men refilled the grave and tied ropes around his wrists. He was taken to a farm where he became a slave with about a hundred other zombies, working in the fields.

American scientists in Haiti studied him in hospital. He had been a zombie for about two years and it was allegedly done on his brother's orders. The brother had had a big argument with Clairvius, so he had called in a *bokor*. Narcisse escaped when the overseer on the farm forgot to give the zombies their daily dose of the drugs which kept them in slavery and subservience. Some of the zombies turned on the overseer and killed him. Narcisse became his normal self but did not want to go back to his village because his brother was there. When he heard in 1980 that his brother had died, he returned to his village, which was called L'Estere. It was eighteen years since he had first been declared dead by his family and friends in the village.

Although zombies are portrayed in horror films as threatening creatures, they are, in fact, helpless beings. Certainly, zombies could kill somebody if they were instructed to do so, but they would not be very efficient at it because they are slow. On the other hand, if a zombie tried to strangle you and you tried to stop it by sticking a knife in it, you could not stop it. You could not frighten a zombie by saying something like: 'I'll shoot you.' If you did shoot it in a vulnerable part, in fact it would die. But whereas if you or I were shot in the arm, we would let go, the zombie would not, because it does not feel very much. Until the zombie was actually dead, it would just continue to do what it had been told.

Mr X said he could handle the physical side of matters, and avoid coming into contact with the poison – and he was fascinated to hear about zombies – but what did I think about the telepathic aspect of it? Could people efficiently curse or not? I think it is utterly certain that you can will people to death. There are numerous stories illustrating similar power. Aleister Crowley, the famous British magician, once spent forty days away from civilization and when he returned, his friends said to him, 'What did you learn?'

He said: 'I'll show you something.' They were walking down Threadneedle Street in London and a chap came out of the Bank of England – a typical city gent with his bowler hat and furled umbrella. Crowley fell into step behind the man and suddenly Crowley dropped down on to one knee and got up again, barely missing a step. The man, who was a few feet ahead of him suddenly tripped and fell over, looked at the ground as if to see what had tripped him, and went on.

That was the story I told the man in Glasgow. This was not a curse in a sense, but it was the power of the will. Cursing, willing – these things overlap. It is the intent that counts. If you intend a thing to happen and if you have enough strong minds aiming in a particular direction, much may be attained. Magic is nothing if not utterly practical. Of course, how is one to know if a curse has really worked or if it is merely coincidence? The British witches always claimed that they stopped Hitler from invading Britain during the Second World War. At the time when he could have invaded, they claimed to have conjured up a column of power and aimed it at him to make him uncertain, so that he would not dare invade – and he did not invade. Now, who knows the truth of it? Wise after the event, anyone can say anything. By virtue of the way magic works, it is almost impossible to get a hundred per cent proof of the truth.

Maybe practitioners who get together can really produce amazing things. I learned at first-hand of a group of occultists in a nearby county who claimed to have committed the perfect murder. They had been double-crossed by a businessman and vowed revenge, so they observed the man's daily activities and discovered that he walked a particular way to work every day, always crossing the road at the same busy junction. The group then rented a room overlooking the junction and met regularly to practise group concentration techniques and to watch the man until the day they decided to act. On this day, the man stood at the edge of the pavement, waiting to cross the busy road, and the group watched silently. A heavy lorry was coming along the road and at a signal, they concentrated hard on the man on the pavement. Suddenly he seemed to lose his balance, to stumble and to fall into the path of the oncoming lorry. The driver had no chance to stop and the man was killed. Was that really murder by telepathy, as they claimed? Or coincidence? It was certainly not a curse which could be explained as self-fulfilling prophecy, for the unfortunate man had no idea of what they intended to do.

But how, Mr X wanted to know, could he defend himself against any possible powers aimed against him? 'You don't have anything to worry about,' I told him. 'There are such things as defence systems.' I told him about some: for example, that he should picture that he had a very bright aura around him, the outside like a mirror, reflecting everything away. 'If anyone sends you a thought that is intended to damage you, they will reflect it back on themselves very severely,' I said. Mr X liked that idea. 'It has an effect as if somebody tries to hit you with a hammer, when you are covered with a thick, impenetrable rubber shield. The hammer would just bounce back and hit the other person.'

'But can I go for them?' Mr X knew who his enemies were and planned to sort them out in a very physical way – but he was worried about their powers. It was clear that their method of battle was to try to freak out the businessmen and gain the upper hand, and they had begun to do it fairly successfully. Were the other group lucky in that completely fortuitously, a number of the victims had become ill? Was it coincidence? Who knows? 'The proof of this pudding will be in the eating,' I said. 'You do as I say and surround yourself with light. Most importantly of all, you are not to worry.' We added that if, on tracking down these opponents, Mr X discovered any witch-bottles, he should make certain to break them all – although I was sure that the idea of some group in Glasgow collecting the *ti bon ange* of an enemy and bottling it up was quite far-fetched.

There is nothing far-fetched about curses, however, and one of the most famous curses was that of Anton le Vey, who ran the Church of Satan in America during the time when Jayne Mansfield was a popular starlet, being groomed to take over from Marilyn Monroe. Jayne Mansfield was a member of Anton le Vey's Satanist group.

Anton le Vey was an ex-police photographer and an ex-circus performer who set himself up as the chief Satanist and wrote a Satanic bible. He was very good at histrionics and kept a pet lion at his house in California where weirdos from all over America would pay a lot of money to attend his ceremonies. Jayne Mansfield's lawyer, Sam Brody, told her that her connection with this occult group was going to damage her reputation, along with her chance of inheriting Marilyn Monroe's crown. The story goes that Anton le Vey was very cross about this and cursed the lawyer. The next day the lawyer had a crash in his car. But still the lawyer did not stop urging Jayne Mansfield to leave the church. In the end, amid much publicity, Anton le Vey openly put a public curse on the lawyer, and warned Jayne Mansfield never to go in the car with him again, or else suffer the consequences. But she did go in the car. A fortnight later, their car crashed into the back of a lorry which had pilings projecting from it. The pilings came straight through the window of the car – and both Jayne Mansfield and her lawyer were decapitated.

That might have been a spooky, modern, Western curse, but cursing is still performed widely throughout the rest of the world. We know the power of suggestion nowadays – the way we feel if a friend tells us we are looking ill or well, just like the old Stanley Holloway song: 'My word, you do look queer!' Here is the essence of the aboriginal curses which involve 'pointing the bone'. The aborigines believe that pointing the bone can have such a fell effect upon a person, that he can literally drop dead with fear there and then. The vital functions stop working and the person may have a huge, explosive burst of adrenalin which sets the heart racing and kills. It used to be thought by Europeans that the only reason the curse worked was because the aborigines believed they were going to die. Now there are many sources which show that you can be cursed and you do not need to know you have been cursed. You are still affected by it. Maybe aborigine people in particular, who are pretty sensitive to psychic effects, are more susceptible. They can, after all, often detect water in hidden places.

But this is a double-edged sword, for this sensitivity enables the aborigines to be affected adversely, also by will. There is a story of two little aborigine girls who were abducted from their village by a man. Their distraught parents eventually got a famous medicine man – who is called a Clever Man in Australia – to come to the village. He pointed a bone in a ceremony which lasted for quite a while, then all of a sudden he stopped pointing it and calmly said: 'Yes, I've got him, I've got him. That's it. Now we wait.' About three days later, two bedraggled, but otherwise healthy, girls staggered out of the undergrowth back into the village. They told of how this chap had abducted them, beaten and assaulted them, probably intending to sell them as slaves to a distant tribe. This continued for two days, then on the third day, he became morose and would not speak. He no longer tried to dominate them and knock them about. That night he became ill and lay still and did not move. They freed themselves from the ropes and he watched them without trying to do anything. The girls ran away. It seemed that this was the moment when the Clever Man had said to their parents: 'I've got him.' From a distance, he had pinpointed and incapacitated the man. So a curse can be effective even if you do not know it has been done. It is not necessarily a self-fulfilling prophecy – although I think it can be both. On the other side of the coin, people who do healing claim they can perform absent healing. They may gather together with other people and 'will' a person better. There is evidence that this works.

I have a friend who is a witch. Her tongue-in-cheek name is Madame Pompadour. She is charming, sophisticated and wealthy, aged about forty-five and single. She knows how to run her life ... helped by magic. She has had many misfortunes and let-downs in her life which have made her bitter towards a number of people, and her attitude is that if anyone lets her down to any degree, she immediately reciprocates, violently. She told me when a boyfriend had abandoned her, and said she felt as if there was a heavy weight on her mind all the time. But she had a spell ready. 'I have pictured that weight going back to him,' she said. 'I picture it as a large safe made of lead, dropping on him.' A week later the ex-boyfriend collapsed with a heart attack. Was it mere coincidence? Are we to deny that she is a very powerful psychic? (*Dare* we deny it?) On another occasion her financial adviser tried to embezzle some of her funds and she was very cross with him, so at once she did one of her spells. Again, within a few days this man had had a heart attack and was forced to retire from his occupation. Any negative sceptic can say what he likes, but it does not alter the fact that this happens every time this particular lady is on the warpath. Her spells seem as reliable as when you press a light-switch and the light goes on.

Magic is as old as the hills. *Real* magic, that is – not the Paul Daniels and David Copperfield stuff. If a person says he or she is a witch, we have to decide what we understand a witch to be. Commonly we mean people who have abilities, who have enough psychic power to make something happen which somebody else could not make happen, by using spells. Fine so far, but this is only a starting-point: there are still many people who are unable to differentiate between black magic and white magic. This is a huge, sprawling field, but to simplify matters, there is one basic difference: white witches, while achieving their objectives, are very careful that they do nothing which can be construed as being aggressive to other people. If they did, this would make them feel guilty, and they believe they would draw back upon themselves divine wrath, from the gods in whom they believe. They are very keen to do 'good', whereas black witchcraft is far more pragmatic. Followers of the so-called left-hand path do whatever they wish to do – whether it hurts anyone else or not – without regard to the consequences. For example, you may believe that you have the power to cast a spell and kill off Auntie Nellie, so inheriting a million pounds. If you are a white witch you will not do it. You will believe it to be wrong and you will fear that there may be some wrath or reciprocation vented upon you. If however, you are a black witch, you will have no hesitation at all in bumping off Auntie Nellie. You will say: 'This is what I want to do; therefore I will do it.' However, this principle applies to more mundane events, too. To make sure you were picked for a particular job, then you might use magic to get it, which is contrary to the widely held belief that black witchcraft is mainly concerned with doing 'evil' things. In black magic, you do things which are practical – and if despatching Auntie Nellie is practical for you, you do that, too, with no qualms. So we can define black and white witches, roughly, as followers of the left- and right-hand paths, the left-hand path being the sinister path, coming from the Latin word *sinister*, which means 'on the left'. It is the anti-clockwise path.

Wicca is the Old English word meaning 'craft of the wise', which has since been changed to witchcraft. Wizard is the Old English word for 'wise man'. The modern movement of witchcraft had a resurgence in Britain after 1951, when the laws against witchcraft were repealed. Witches believe in the deity Diana and her daughter Aradia. Lucifer is Diana's 'husband' – he is a quite different Lucifer from the Christian Lucifer who is believed to be a fallen angel. Witchcraft differs from the Christian-Judaic religious tradition in being a maternalistic rather than a paternalistic religion. They have God the Mother, rather than God the Father. The great goddess requires no sacrifice of any sort. She is a loving goddess, a mother-goddess; she is mother nature and mother earth.

Dr Margaret Murray considered that witchcraft was a real, animistic religion that antedated all others. An animistic religion means that everything is thought to have an in-dwelling spirit: every tree, every stone, every animal, every plant and every stream has a spirit in it. The spirits of the trees were known as dryads – the ancient Greeks called them the hamadryads. The belief was that if you chopped the tree down, the hamadryad would die also. The spirits of plants were called devas. In the Moray Firth of Scotland the Findhorn Society claimed that it was their contact with the spirits of the plants which enabled them to grow huge vegetables. They would talk to the plants and would probably say that when you talk to your plants, as Prince Charles does, what is really happening is not so much that the plant is listening to you, but that the devas listen and they are happy to be given your attention. Therefore they encourage the plant to grow.

The biggest mistake which many people make is believing that witches have something to do with Satanists. That is completely wrong. A Satanist is, by definition, someone who worships Satan, which gives him more in common with Christians than witches, because Satan, or Mephistopheles, or Beelzebub – call him what you will – is the Christian Devil. White and black witches don't believe in Satan any more than they believe in Jesus. These are separate belief systems. Satanists, too, come in all shapes and sizes. Once, after I had written a newspaper article about Anton le Vey and Satanism, the newspaper received an angry letter from the Temple of Set, saying: 'We are the real Satanists.' Set was the evil brother of Osiris, the good Egyptian god, and it was Set who had Osiris murdered. Like any religion, to the people who believe in it, this is not mythology; it is true. The Temple of Set in England apparently call themselves the Chief Satanists of England and this chap wrote, saying: 'Robin Furman has been reading too much Dennis Wheatley. The head Satanist was not Anton le Vey. The Temple of Set is the leading Satanic group.' Set or Satan? This is like saying that a Christian worships Christ and then finding you have Protestants, Catholics and Christian Scientists. You might say, how can they all be different if they are all the same? And it is the same in Satanism. The people in the

Temple of Set say they're not going to worship any Christian invention, so they will worship Set. It depends on whom you choose.

I have been at meetings of covens and it is very much like going to church, except that at some covens people take their clothes off, and at others they do not. The black groups are into sex in a big way, and will use sex as a force and a power, which, of course, it is. On one occasion, back in 1980, my friend Simon, who used to work at the university where I was doing research, and who is the high priest of a white group in Yorkshire, invited myself and another friend from university along to a ceremony at his house, to see what it was like. Simon and his wife were both witches and there were some girls there from the university, plus a couple of other chaps from Hull, one of whom had a girl with him. It was the sort of coven where you stripped off – or as they put it, went 'sky-clad'.

At this ceremony, the witches were very keen on trying to help friends and harm no one. They cast a few spells to help. Black witches help their friends too, of course, but they are unconcerned about harming anyone – and black magic involves even more sex, as I was to discover when I went along to such a ceremony. Curiously enough, I was invited by a man whom I met in a supermarket! We were queuing at the check-out desk and he suddenly said: 'Aren't you Robin Furman? I saw you in the paper the other night.' We started chatting and went for a coffee in the supermarket, which is when he told me about the group he belonged to. 'We're having a ceremony tomorrow, at a friend's house,' he said. 'Would you like to come?' It all sounded fascinating.

'Why not?' I said, and so it was arranged. As we went our different ways in the car park, he turned back to me.

'We're not white witches, you know,' he said. 'But we aren't Satanists, either.' I wondered what I would find when I arrived.

The following evening I met him and his friend at the pre-arranged spot and we went to a house in an old residential district of Grimsby. We walked up the driveway of an old semi-detached house with heavy curtains at the windows, which were drawn. There were cloaks prepared for us. We went into a cloakroom and undressed, putting on these monk-like cloaks, and then entered the living room, which had been transformed into a place of worship. A sweet and heavy smell hung on the atmosphere: there was incense burning. The high priest entered. He wore a cloak embroidered with various designs: an inverted pentagram, together with various words of power in 'shorthand'. They were just letters from Greek, Hebrew and Latin. These things are amalgams from many sources and judging from the symbols, I guessed that the group probably used words like Belthagor, Leviathon and Melchar in their spells and enchantment. These are the names of demonic entities, known from the times of King Solomon, and you do not have to be a Satanist to use these words. However, you do have to be somebody who is quite happy to use the powers of evil. Aleister Crowley, one of Britain's most famous magicians, apparently conjured up another demonic entity called Choronzon, and according to the report, it escaped from the circle in which it was supposed to stay, and got to Crowley, taking over his body and driving him mad. In Crowley's body, it tried to kill Victor Neuberg, who was helping Crowley, but with others, Neuberg managed to overpower Crowley, who was locked up for six months until he recovered. The same thing happened to Dennis Wheatley, who also spent six months in a retreat. After that, he always included a footnote to his books, saying that he did not practise black magic and would not recommend anyone else to practise.

The high priest's robe also had a cowl-hood, and his face was in shadow. Then a woman came in and lay on the dining table. She was wearing a black robe, and with a few words to the powers-that-be, with the waving of swords and other items, the girl was stripped off. Underneath her robe she was wearing loose garments which were easily removed. One of the men had a bell which he rang as each item of clothing was taken off. The girl was very pretty and appeared to enjoy it immensely. Whether it had anything to do with magic or not is another matter. She was spreadeagled naked on the table and the bell clanged mournfully. Everyone turned as one of the members entered the room, carrying a chalice of wine. Slowly he brought it to the table and the chalice was carefully placed upon her pudenda and held there as she was anointed with it. Signs were made upon her head and breasts with wet fingers. It was at this point that everybody began to strip off. The scent of the incense filled the room as the coven members began chanting, asking for energies to fill the woman. The group, which called itself the Brotherhood of Isis, sent messages to Osiris and Isis of ancient Egypt. One cannot see how that can be applicable to everyday events in the twentieth century, but nevertheless, this is what the group did.

When the woman arose from the table, she was somebody else – or so the group believed. The spirit of a princess of ancient Egypt was now possessing the body that had been on the table – and the woman was acting very well. I learned that the Brotherhood of Isis went in for flagellation as well as the naked ceremonies and there were two young fellows who were to be initiated that night. They were naked, as were we all, and they were plucked from the circle and bound, hand and foot. 'Kneel!' they were ordered, and they knelt before the high priest with their heads on the ground. The woman who was taking the part of the high priestess had to do the flagellating across the buttocks of the young men. She used a rod with silken tassels on the end. It was supposed to be a token flagellation, but she certainly got into the spirit of the thing. I heard her say to one of the other girls: 'Do you know, I could really get to like this!'

After this excitement, it was downhill all the way for an observer like me. There was some more boring ceremonial. The two men who had been initiated were sworn to secrecy. There were spells cast, calling upon entities and spirits to ensure jobs for the girls and punishment for somebody who had upset the group. They cursed the offender and said the person – an ex-member – was to fade away unless he left the group alone. 'Do whatever is necessary. Anything at all,' they said – which is something you would not hear in a white group.

On yet another occasion, I was invited to go to a devil-worshipping ceremony and I asked what they did. 'We don't have human sacrifices, but there might be a few cats,' they said. I declined the invitation. 'Of course, it's regrettable but necessary, because you have energy in the blood and it's part of the ceremony,' they explained.

I said: 'You may be perfectly right – but it isn't necessary for me.' We parted on good terms, which I believe was a very sensible move on my part. Much public hysteria has been whipped up recently about Satanism and child abuse. The 1990 case in Rochdale was one in point, when more than thirty children who lived on a council estate were removed from their parents because social workers suspected that they were involved in Satanic ceremonies. Whatever the truth of that incident, child sexual abuse is not the norm among black-magic practitioners. However, many people become black magicians or Satanists, not because they are particularly into black magic and the Devil, but because it gives them an excuse to indulge their own sordid preferences.

The same principle applies elsewhere. Aleister Crowley did not class himself as either a witch or a Satanist, but a practitioner of Magik, a sorcerer or a magician. He was unconcerned about a Christian God, and he did not worship the Devil. He did not worship anything, but would perform the appropriate rites to conjure up forces as he saw them, which is different to genuflecting before them. When Crowley was a boy, he went to a horrible church school where they beat him unmercifully. His parents belonged to a sect called the Plymouth Brethren and he was beaten regularly in the name of Jesus. As they applied fifteen strokes with a large, heavy cane they would say: 'One stroke for Jesus. Two strokes for Jesus,' and so on. Quite understandably, Crowley was left with an enduring detestation of Jesus and Christianity for the rest of his life.

Crowley believed he could conjure up magical effects and I'm sure one can. But does anyone know the forces with which they are working? It is very easy to deny that something works, just as it is very easy to delude yourself into believing that something works. As Ghostbusters, we explain to people what we are doing in the most practical way possible, and it can be seen with modern instrumentation, but we are not afraid of being open-minded about something and saying: 'We do not know what this effect is, but we'll handle it in whichever way we possibly can.

Perhaps you recall Yorkie Steve from Chapter 4, the Wonderland worker who was one of the people who saw a ghost in the former indoor fairground. On my first visit to Wonderland, he told me a fascinating story about a witch who had saved his small daughter's life several years previously. Steve was a miner at the time and was separated from his wife. He bought a little cottage in a village called Edwinston, a place where, apparently, there was a lot of devil worship and there had been problems with desecration at the church. The cottage had cost Steve only £13,000, which was very cheap, even in those days. Then he learned why it was so cheap: he was told by someone in the village that the cottage had stood empty because it was haunted and no one would buy it. Close to the cottage was a place called Black Hills Farm, which was owned by a woman called Sheila Doyle. 'Black Hills Farm was supposed to be built over an old witch burial ground,' said Steve. 'There have been lots of strange things that have happened there, such as a bedroom which was found to be covered in frost, when the weather was warm.' Sheila was known as a powerful psychic and had also discovered that the house was built on the crossing point of eleven ley lines. Steve's house was the end one in a terrace of cottages. 'Everyone who had lived there before had divorced,' Steve said. He had moved in with his girlfriend. 'It wasn't long after we moved in that strange things started happening. We heard rappings on the bedroom wall that sounded like machine-gun fire. The noise lasted for about twelve seconds at a time.'

For whatever reason, whether it was because of the strange noises, or whether the relationship hit problems, Steve's girlfriend left the cottage and Steve stayed at the house for six more months with no trouble at all. Then Steve's ex-wife, Jackie, turned up and moved in with him. 'She came home one day and suddenly accused me of having another woman in the house,' he said. 'It just wasn't true – but there was a strong smell of expensive perfume in the sitting room. Then when we went to bed, something touched Jackie – twice.' Jackie felt an invisible hand brush back her hair and then it touched her breast.

'Things went missing,' said Yorkie Steve. 'Once, my cigarettes and matches just vanished from the side of the chair where I was sitting. I went to the shop and bought some more, then I went to make a cup of tea. I opened the fridge and there were the cigarettes and matches that had been lost. Lots of other things disappeared – and we kept smelling perfume.' Jackie became pregnant and had a little boy, Peter. On the day he was born Steve returned from the hospital to find that all the shelves in the house were smashed. Subsequently they had a little girl, Tina, who became very sickly. This was perhaps not surprising, for the house seemed to be getting colder and colder and there was a smell of damp. No matter what they tried to do, they could not warm it up. 'We had two dogs and they began to refuse to go into the baby's bedroom,' said Steve. 'She was really pretty ill. She couldn't keep any food down at all, not even the special food that the hospital had given us for her. She got weaker and weaker and it really seemed as if the baby was dying. Then one day, there was a knock on the door and when I opened it, there was Sheila, the woman who owned Black Hills Farm.

' "I know your baby is dying," she told me. "It's because your house is haunted – but I can fix it for you." I wouldn't let her in at first. She was middle-aged, with long black hair – she looked a bit of a weirdo, to say the least. But on the other hand, Tina really was so very ill. Anything was worth a try.' Sheila told Steve to make everyone leave the house and told them not to attempt to enter again, no matter what happened. 'She was in there for about twenty minutes and when she came out she was drenched in sweat,' said Steve. 'She said it was the worst house she had ever exorcized, that she had driven out four ghosts, but that one remained to act as a "guardian". We went back in and the house, which had been so cold and damp, was warm. It smelt as if it had been spring-cleaned. More importantly, the baby made a full recovery. It was like magic.' Steve got to know Sheila quite well after this. There is a witch circle at Rufford Abbey nearby and Steve once saw a man with a grey-painted face, black lips and black cloak chanting in his garden and looking up at his son's bedroom window. He thought this was probably because of his friendship with Sheila who, he said, used to go out to the abbey and remove from the ground evil totems that had been placed there for black-magic ceremonies, replacing them with good ones. 'They didn't like Sheila because of this,' he explained, 'but the magic didn't seem to affect her.' In fact, Sheila made several predictions about Steve's future, including that he would give up mining after ten years to run his own business (he had a pub in Chesterfield). She also predicted the divorce which would split the family – Steve kept Peter and his wife Jackie kept Tina – and that he would go to live by the sea in Humberside. And so it came to pass that Yorkie Steve ultimately came to Wonderland.

Perhaps witchcraft contributed to the grim happenings at a 250-year-old pump cottage in North Cockerington, a small village in Lincolnshire. Ian and Jill Lock had been delighted to find this little character cottage with an acre of garden on the main road (although in a village like North Cockerington, the 'main road' was more like a village lane), and they bought it at a good price, for it had been standing empty for three years. Once they had agreed to buy, the previous owner told them that the key was on a piece of string hanging behind the door – and he fled. 'You can keep everything in the house,' he said, and he meant *everything*. There was a microwave and a computer left behind; a deep-fat fryer and even personal objects such as clothes in a wardrobe and a photograph album. Ian and Jill immediately began to 'do up' the cottage, for it was certainly in a primitive state – the kitchen plumbing consisted of a tap stuck in the wall and little else. The couple started their renovations. Oak beams were planned for the living-room ceiling and they began knocking two rooms into one to create a spacious kitchen. They began extending downstairs and rebuilding bedrooms upstairs. They put in new floors and windows. Then came the day when a local passer-by stopped for a chat with the new villagers. 'You do know that the cottage is haunted, don't you?' said the local.

That did not do Jill and Ian any good at all, for they had been experiencing odd events which until now they had put out of their minds. Doors opened and closed on their own, door-handles moved and objects in the house were felt to go hot and cold. 'Something' had sat on the bed of one of their sons. The events became worse and their boys, Sean and Simon, aged nine and twelve, were becoming very frightened. One day, Sean came home from school and heard the cottage door slam. Then he saw someone dimly through the windows. Too scared to go in by himself, he called a neighbour to go in with him. There was nobody in the house. On another occasion, water came through the wall of the house, but when the plumber was called in, he could find no explanation for why this had happened. When the Ghostbusters were called in Ian and Jill were reaching the point of blind terror. Late one night they had heard an almighty thump, 'like a sack of flour being dropped from a great height', on the ceiling. They ran upstairs. It came from the boys' bedroom and when they went into the room, Simon was sitting up in bed, screaming, with staring eyes. But as they went to comfort him, the screams turned to hysterical laughter and Simon seemed to be in a trance-like state as he laughed madly, staring ahead, Ian and Jill had shivered in horror. When they had woken and calmed their young son, he had no memory of either crying or laughing. Then there was the behaviour of the family's two dogs, which had become most peculiar. They both became incontinent and the vet could find no reason for this. The dogs refused to go upstairs in the cottage or into one of the rooms. One dog was found huddled in a corner, terrified. Unable to cope with the dogs' incontinence, Jill and Ian gave away their dogs to a friend. The animals recovered at once. It was after the dogs had gone that the family began to hear the growling. 'It was like an animal growling around the kitchen area,' Jill told the Ghostbusters when we arrived. 'It was a gargling sort of noise. And it isn't just we who have heard it. A friend of our son heard the growling when he arrived at the house one day – and he wouldn't come in!'

One night the family were in bed – the two boys were sharing one bedroom while renovations went on in another. Ian said: 'Suddenly, I heard the most awful gurgling, growling, howling sound. It was a noise that I never want to hear again. It was coming from downstairs. It was like a wild animal growling with water in its throat, a most blood-curdling sound, horribly weird. I went downstairs to see what it was, and there was nothing there.'

'My nerves are completely on edge,' said Jill. 'I really don't think I'm going to be able to stay in the house. We're going to have to move out.' Our machinery confirmed that there were indeed various energy changes taking place around the house. The Probe recorded temperature changes and in certain parts of the house there was a feeling of pressure in one's ears. This may not have been owing to any ghostly phenomena, but it could well have been this pressure which had disturbed the dogs.

'But what,' I asked as we went around the cottage, 'is the ghost story surrounding this place?' It seemed that the cottage was inhabited at some time in its history by a woman who was known as the local witch. She used to make up medicines and herbal remedies. She was also the village prostitute. The men would come home from their sea voyages and go with her. Then they discovered that the woman had 'the pox' – a venereal disease – but she was still sleeping with the men. They were furious, and the story goes that one night the villagers got together and strangled her in the house. This was the grisly story which Ian and Jill were told. If the energies of this hapless woman were still around Pump Cottage, perhaps a seance would be the best way to settle it, we thought to ourselves.

The following evening we arrived, armed with our ouija 'Talking Board'. The ouija is so named because it means 'yes' in both French and German – *'oui'* and *'ja'*. Our board is a Waddington's brand and contains a planchette – a little heart-shaped pointer on three stumpy legs. The board has an illustrated 'Yes' and 'No' together with the letters of the alphabet and the numbers one to nine. It also has 'Goodbye' on one side. In the darkened room, we all placed a finger on the planchette and waited. Slowly it began to move. Ian and Jill held their breath. 'Who is this?' we asked, and a word was spelt out: Mary. Was the murdered witch-prostitute called Mary? We hadn't a clue. 'Mary' told us that things were unhappy here many years ago. The messages were intermittent and far from satisfactory, but Jill and Ian were very keen and seemed pleased, although we thought the success was minimal. We addressed 'Mary': 'It's OK, you can stay here if you want,' we said, 'but you can move on. You are not tied here. We are not the people who were antagonistic to you.' Was 'Mary' really the witch-prostitute? Were we conversing with a ghost? Or were the responses being caused by some sort of externalized energy produced by the people in the house? Strong emotions can hold a haunt in place and keep it going. Was the 'spirit' moving the planchette – or could it be exerting telepathic power to influence human energies and in a subtle way cause a person to make the movements on the board on its behalf? Then again, someone can simply move the planchette unconsciously. It might be at the behest of a spirit, but then again, it might not. There is such a thing as unconscious muscular activity, but since it is unconscious, that lends weight to the view that the unconscious *might* be influenced by external sources.

We considered the facts: Ian and Jill's boys had been in an emotional state; they were the children of Jill's first marriage and although they seemed to interact well with Ian, there may have been underlying problems of adjustment which they would have to make. It was my view that the emotional pressure was increased by the boys sharing a bedroom. There is much telepathic bonding between two brothers who are so close in age. Experiments have been performed in the United States at the Maimonedes Dream Laboratory in which one person sleeps while another concentrates on a picture. The idea is to see if one person can influence another's dreaming mind – and it has been shown that people who are close can do this. If Pump Cottage was a haunted site, perhaps the effects would have been minimal until something happened to activate the haunt. Empty houses are not often haunted. It seems that, at the very least, these psychic energies need a living being to allow them to manifest to a greater or lesser extent. Even Raudive – who, you may recall, advocated leaving a tape-recorder switched on in an empty room to record voices from another dimension – found he had better results if he also left his Great Dane dog in the room with the tape-recorder.

I suggested that when the second bedroom was ready for the Lock sons, the effects would diminish – and this proved to be the case. The cottage is now pleasantly quiet. It is still possible to detect energies at one part of the house, but not to a disturbing extent. Each case is different. Maybe we did encounter a disembodied ghost and with our seance we performed a secular exorcism. Maybe this is too simple a solution. Whatever caused the effects, they are now fading away.

The Ghostbusters are not here to preach to anyone. It makes no difference to us whether people believe in ghosts or not. We don't mind about flat-earthers or sceptics. We just know that people are usually very pleased to see us. The paranormal is one of the most widely read about and studied subjects around today. It remains an area of controversy and interest, and outside the celluloid Ghostbusters we are the only serious group of scientific amateur Ghostbusters in the world who are immediately recognized by the public. This has brought us minor notoriety.

What do we say to people who dismiss poltergeists, ghosts and the like as simply the products of over-imagination? Those sceptics who say that the victims of hauntings are just making things up?

We say: 'Fine. But when you get one ... who are you going to call?'

Bibliography

Berlitz, Charles, *Without a Trace* (Panther, London 1978)

Blum, Ralph and Judy, *Beyond Earth*, (Corgi Books, London 1974)

Calkins, Carroll C. (ed) *Mysteries of the Unexplained* (The Reader's Digest Association, Inc., New York, Montreal 1982)

Encyclopedia of Witchcraft and Demonology (Octopus Books Ltd, London 1974)

David-Neel, Alexandra, *Magic and Mystery in Tibet* (Souvenir Press, London 1967)

Eysenck, Hans J., and Sargent, Carl, *Explaining the Unexplained* (Weidenfeld and Nicolson, London 1982)

Fodor, Nandor, *Between Two Worlds* (West Nyack, New York; Parker Publishing Company Inc. 1964)

Inglis, Brian, *The Paranormal: An Encyclopedia of Psychic Phenomena* (Granada Publishing, London 1985)

Inglis, Brian, *The Hidden Power* (Cape, London 1986)

Lord Kilbraken, *Tell Me The Next One* (V. Gollancz Ltd., London 1950)

Manchester, Sean, 'The Highgate Vampire', in *The Vampire's Bedside Companion* (Leslie Frewin Ltd, London 1975)

Manning, Matthew, *The Link* (Colin Smythe Ltd, London 1974)

Monroe, Robert, *Journeys Out of the Body* (Doubleday, US, 1971; Souvenir Press, London 1972)

Moss, Thelma, *The Probability of the Impossible: Scientific Discoveries and Explorations in the Psychic World* (J.P. Tacher, Los Angeles 1974)

Ostrander, Sheila, and Shroeder, Lynn, *Psi, Psychic Discoveries Behind the Iron Curtain* (Abacus, London 1973)

Owen, I., and Sparrow, M., *Conjuring Up Philip* (Harper and Row, New York 1976)

Pedlar, Kit, *Mind Over Matter* (Eyre Methuen, London 1981)

Playfair, Guy Lyon, *This House is Haunted. An Investigation of the Enfield Poltergeist* (Souvenir Press, London 1980)

Radnor, Alan, *Paranormal or Normal?* (Lennard Publishing, London 1989)

Randles, Jenny, *Beyond Explanation?* (Robert Hale, London 1985)

Underwood, Peter (ed) *Dictionary of the Occult and Supernatural* (George G. Harrap Ltd., London 1978)

Welfare, Simon, and Fairley, John, *Arthur C. Clarke's Mysterious World* (Collins, London 1980)

White, Alan, *Philosophy of Mind* (Random House, New York 1967)

Wilson, Colin, *Poltergeist! A Study in Destructive Haunting* (New English Library, London 1981)

Wilson, Colin, *Beyond the Occult: Twenty Years' Research into the Paranormal* (Bantam Press, London 1988)